D0723477

TOGETHER WE BUILD

338.761
J71t

TOGETHER WE BUILD

The Life and Faith of Wallace E. Johnson

by Wallace E. Johnson
with Eldon Roark

338.7616*7940924

HAWTHORN BOOKS, INC.
Publishers/New York
A Howard & Wyndham Company

53654

For a bookplate autographed by the author and a "goal card," write
to: Wallace E. Johnson, P.O. Box 18127, Memphis, Tenn. 38118

TOGETHER WE BUILD

Copyright © 1978, 1973 by Wallace E. Johnson–E. B. McCool
Foundation. Copyright under International and Pan-American
Copyright Conventions. All rights reserved, including the right to
reproduce this book or portions thereof in any form, except for the
inclusion of brief quotations in a review. All inquiries should be
addressed to Hawthorn Books, Inc., 260 Madison Avenue, New York,
New York 10016. This book was manufactured in the United States
of America and published simultaneously in Canada by Prentice-
Hall of Canada, Limited, 1870 Birchmount Road, Scarborough,
Ontario.

Previously published as *Work Is My Play*

Library of Congress Catalog Card Number: 77–090091

ISBN: 0–8015–8851–0

3 4 5 6 7 8 9 10

Contents

Foreword

Here in *Together We Build* is what you have been looking for—an interesting, easily read, modern Horatio Alger story. It is a motivational guide to success in achieving your personal, family, or business goals, whether you are a teen-age student, sales representative, clerk, factory worker, entrepreneur, chairman of an international conglomerate, or housewife.

Wallace Johnson was a youth, born in poverty, who acquired great wealth and is esteemed by hundreds of thousands of persons for his business, philanthropic, and religious activities. Unlike many authors of biographies, he tells you how he achieved his success by employing universal principles that will help you, me, and everyone else reach our goals if we apply those that are applicable to us. Most, if not all, of them are. I know from experience, for they are listed in *The Success System That Never Fails*, which I authored, and *Success Through a Positive Mental Attitude*, which I coauthored with Napoleon Hill. And that's why I know that *Together We Build* can be a self-help guide for you.

It will be relatively easy for you to recognize those universal principles and to see how they were applied step by step, what action was taken by Wally to reach his predetermined objectives, and how you can use these fundamental laws that guarantee success. All you need to do when reading the book is to underscore the philosophy, principles, and quotations memorized by the author, then review the text and study the underscoring, and write down and memorize those quotations and formulas that appeal to you, so that they will flash from your subconscious to your conscious mind in time of need. When one of them does, immediately follow through with action. It is important that you write out your goals and that you review them daily.

Wallace Johnson, in his own interesting style, explains how he uses the same principles that Napoleon Hill and I have used to motivate the tens of thousands of persons who have been exposed to our writings, lectures, records, audiotapes, videotapes, and movies. The lives of countless thousands were changed for the better because they responded by motivating themselves to achieve their goals. *Together We Build* can be a self-help guide to personal achievement to motivate you to motivate yourself and convert your dreams and desires into reality.

Take particular note of Wallace Johnson's (1) burning desires, (2) positive mental attitudes, (3) particularly high goal setting, (4) thinking and planning time, (5) self-discipline, (6) initiative, (7) enthusiasm, (8) controlled attention, (9) creative imagination, (10) budgeting of time and money, (11) maintaining good physical and mental health, (12) selection of a mastermind group consisting of his wife, Alma, and partners like Kemmons Wilson, who worked in harmony to help him achieve his objectives, (14) teamwork with his partners and associates, (15) ability to turn adversities into seeds of equivalent or greater benefits, (16) willingness to go the extra mile, and (17) application of his faith. Particularly count the number of times Wallace Johnson communicated with his unseen Senior Silent Partner, the One he had in mind when he titled his work *Together We Build*.

W. CLEMENT STONE

Preface

Why should a man write a book about his life?

Well, that's a good question. I can't answer it for others —only for myself.

Many friends have said to me, "Wallace, you should write a book about your life. You and your partner, Kemmons Wilson, have had unusual careers, and you are good examples of what poor boys can do in this great country under our free-enterprise system. Your story would be an inspiration to others."

And you know how it is. If enough people keep telling you something, you get to believing it.

At the risk of seeming immodest, I must agree that I have come quite a way from my humble beginning in a Mississippi sharecropper's cottage. But I didn't do it alone. I've had help from many sources along the way—help from God, help from a pretty and levelheaded wife, help from the finest businessman in America as a partner, help from kind and capable friends and associates.

I am not a genius, and I make no claims to brilliance. What success I have achieved can be attained by others— if they are willing to pay the price. It can mean long hours of hard work and study, and the foregoing of many activities that most people consider pleasure.

Sometimes people—young people in particular—ask me to give them some rules for success. Well, every person is different in personality and ability, so that's a tough order. What worked for me at a certain time may not work for others. We live in a fast-changing world. But in this book I do point out some truths that never change, which always will be reliable guidelines.

Another reason for writing this book is that I enjoyed reliving my life. It has been fun to remember and put down in writing my big moments, not only the wins but the losses and the draws. Strange how the pleasant experiences seem to dwarf the failures, disappointments and frustrations. Many things that are harsh and unpleasant when they happen become soft and humorous when seen from the perspective of time.

And a further reason for this book—and I might as well be honest about it—is that it pleases me to think that others may want to read about my life. If you can find in it something entertaining, a little practical advice and a bit of inspiration, I shall feel that it was worthwhile.

And finally I wanted to write this book as my testimonial to the greatness and goodness of God, who has done so much for me.

Memphis, Tennessee   W.E.J.

TOGETHER WE BUILD

1

IT WAS

KEMMONS'

IDEA

I was going over some papers on my desk, figuring out financial and work schedules for some of my home-building projects and, as I look back now, I think I was a little irritated by the ringing of the phone. Why did people call me at home at night when I was so accessible during working hours?

Without looking up from a column of figures I off-handedly answered, "Hello."

"Hello, Wallace? This is Kemmons Wilson."

Kemmons was a bright young businessman who had made quite a name for himself in home construction, real estate, apartment houses, theaters, vending machines. We were friends but had not been associated in any deals or projects.

We exchanged pleasantries and then he got to the point.

"I've got a business idea that I think might interest you. Are you busy?"

"You mean tonight?" I asked.

"Yes, I'd like to come over."

I hesitated. The work on my desk needed to be finished.

Yet there was enthusiasm in Kemmons' voice, and people who are enthusiastic get to me.

"Why, of course, Kemmons, come on over."

A few minutes later we were seated opposite each other and he was telling me about his idea.

"Wallace," he said, "I want you to be my partner in the motel business. A chain across the nation."

He said he knew of my experience and success in the construction fields and knew of my connection with the National Home Builders Association. He thought we'd hit it off together just fine as partners and felt that home builders would be just the people to work with in establishing a chain of quality motels at reasonable prices.

I felt greatly honored and was pleased. Kemmons had already made a good start in the business.

About two years previously he and his family had made a vacation tour, and he had come back with his dander up. He was both astonished and outraged by the poor accommodations they had found and the high prices they had to pay. It had cost him ten dollars a night for Mrs. Wilson and himself, plus two or three dollars extra for each of their five children. The motels were hot, dirty, noisy. Rooms were so small they had no place to sit. Some bathrooms were no larger than little closets, and often the plumbing fixtures were loud and defective.

Many motels did not have restaurants, or, if they did, the restaurants were unsanitary and served tasteless or unpalatable food that not even tired and hungry travelers could stomach.

Motel operators didn't seem to realize the war was over, and people were no longer satisfied to pay high prices for any kind of accommodations.

Kemmons was so disgusted over conditions that he determined to build the kinds of motels he and his family would enjoy stopping at. And he went to it without delay. He built a 120-unit on Summer Avenue in Memphis near the eastern city limits and called it Holiday Inn. Later, he built three more in good locations around the city. He put into them comforts and conveniences he had found lacking in motels on their miserable trip—air-conditioning, bright and spacious rooms, phones with twenty-four-hour switchboard service, adequate bathrooms with plumbing in good condition, free ice, plenty of parking space, dog kennels, swimming pools. All his motels had restaurants. And he had kept prices within reason.

His mother, Mrs. Ruby Lloyd Wilson, better known to all her friends as "Doll," a cute, vivacious and talented little woman, had been his close associate in the venture, just as she had been in other big deals and projects throughout his career. She was his decorator, and many of the attractive features of the motels were her ideas. (She later became a Holiday Inn vice-president and was a great inspiration.)

Yes, Kemmons had proved some things to his own satisfaction and was off to a good start in the motel business. But he had always been a big thinker and wasn't satisfied with small success. He was on fire with enthusiasm. He felt there was a great opportunity in America for a chain of quality motels that charged fair prices.

He would have rooms as low as four dollars a night—that was in 1953, remember—and there would be no charge for children under twelve. Motels in the chain would have good, clean restaurants, swimming pools and all the other luxuries and conveniences he had put into his first four. Porters would be available for people who wanted them, but they would not force themselves on guests at every turn, with hands annoyingly outstretched for tips.

And Kemmons was convinced that his motels should be built out on the highways on the edges of towns, away from heavy city traffic—out where travelers could sit in front of their units on pleasant nights and look up at the stars and relax after dinner and then go in to a comfortable bed and get a good night's rest in preparation for another day on the road.

As he gave me his ideas for a national chain of motels, I caught his enthusiasm. We sat way past bedtime, kicking ideas around. We would offer travelers the same high quality wherever they went, he said. We would make reservations for them at other inns ahead on the trip, without cost to them. If businessmen wanted to have conferences with other businessmen, we would provide adequate meeting rooms.

"How would you go about raising capital?" I asked.

Kemmons had thought this phase through, too, as he had most aspects of the venture. I was intrigued—and game. Right there, that night, we agreed to become partners. We would build some motels of our own, and we would sell franchises to others who wanted to join us in carrying out our ideas. We felt that by licensing others we could get national coverage rapidly and thus make our referral and reservation system more effective and our advertising campaign more productive.

It was nearly two A.M. when I walked Kemmons out to his car.

"By the way, what would you call these inns?" I asked.

"I'd name them the same as I did my first one on Summer Avenue—Holiday Inn."

"Sounds good to me," I said.

Kemmons said good night and drove out the driveway.

As I turned to go back in, I rolled those four syllables around on my tongue—"Holiday Inn . . . Holiday Inn."

It did have a good sound.

2

When I think back to the beginning of Holiday Inns, it's hard for me to stop there, because the real beginning for me goes back considerably further. Without some other important steps I'd never have been in a position to join Kemmons with his dream. No, life doesn't work that way.

Some people read a beautiful poem, listen to a great symphony orchestra, stand in frozen awe and admiration before a great masterpiece of sculpture—and are never the same again. Their lives are profoundly touched.

I, too, have had that kind of experience. My life also has been strongly influenced by a fine piece of art—a kissing bridge. Up to the time I saw it, I couldn't make up my mind what I wanted to be: a farmer, a lumberjack or a locomotive engineer. But after I saw Uncle Emmett's kissing bridge—after I heard folks talk about what a marvel it was and tell how people came from far away to see and study it —there never again was any doubt in my mind as to what I would become.

I was going to be a carpenter, a contractor, a builder. I was going to construct bridges, houses, great buildings. My destiny was settled.

I was nine years old.

Do you know what a kissing bridge is? Well, that's what people jokingly called covered bridges years ago, back in the horse-and-buggy days. Young fellows out with their girls for a ride on Sunday afternoons sometimes would stop in the seclusion of a covered bridge and steal a kiss. And traffic being as light as it was then, it often could be a rather prolonged kiss before anybody else came along.

Bridges in those days, however, weren't covered to promote romance. That was just a fringe benefit. The reason they were covered was to protect the timbers from the weather and to save the taxpayers money. A roof over a bridge served the same purpose as a roof over a house.

My birthplace, Edinburg, Mississippi, is on Pearl River. Before I was born and during my early childhood, a number of attempts were made to bridge the river there. But nobody had been able to build a bridge that would stand for long. A flood would come sweeping down the Pearl, and away the bridge would go. People would have to go back to crossing the river on a little ferry, which, of course, was a slow business even to farmers used to a buggy pace.

But county officials were determined to have a bridge, and they kept trying. And my Uncle Emmett, my father's brother, said, by golly, he would build a bridge that would stand, come hell or high water.

He was a carpenter and all-'round mechanic, just as my father and other Johnson men were, and he got a book called *Radford's Estimator* and studied it. It was a handbook for construction men. Told you how to estimate the cost of jobs, the kinds of materials to use, and gave bits of engineering advice and all that sort of thing.

Uncle Emmett studied the book, and he got out a pencil and figured and drew plans. He designed a covered bridge that would hold itself up by its own bootstraps, so to speak, without the need of any undersupports out in the water. He hadn't had any engineering schooling and didn't know how to figure stresses and strains, but he was a natural-born engineer. He just knew how much weight a truss of a certain size could support.

Well, Uncle Emmett built that covered bridge, and, just as he had promised, it stood, come hell or high water. It seemed half a mile long to my wide, boyish eyes, but everything seemed much bigger then, the river, the creeks, the sawmills and gins. As I look back with mature eyes through more than half a century, I see Uncle Emmett's wonder bridge as about 150 feet long. I have no way of checking the accuracy of my memory, for the bridge has been gone many years. I might add, though, that progress, not high water, destroyed it. It could stand the pressure of everything against it, except the pressure of a modern highway system. During the years that it stood, people never ceased to marvel at it. A bridge holding itself up without supports!

Members of our family naturally gloried in Uncle Emmett's feat and fame. And there was an extra bit of triumph for him and for us in his construction of the bridge.

When the county decided to make one more try at bridging Pearl River, officials asked for bids. Uncle Emmett put in a bid, but he wasn't low man. Another bidder was low and got the contract. And then he found himself stuck and embarrassed. He didn't know how to construct such a big and difficult bridge and had to hire Uncle Emmett to build it.

I don't know whether he had to pay Uncle Emmett more than the bid and lost money on the project, or whether Uncle Emmett worked for less than he had originally asked and helped the contractor get off the hook. But that's unimportant. The big thing is that Uncle Emmett designed and built a bridge that stood when many people said it couldn't be done.

And, as I have explained, it was a tremendous thing in my life, for it crystallized my ambitions. It made me want to be a great builder like Uncle Emmett.

I won't say I wouldn't have become a builder if it hadn't been for Uncle Emmett and his kissing bridge, for I believe I was destined to be a carpenter and contractor from birth, but it was the nudge that I needed. I believe I am what I am because God answered my parents' prayers and my own prayers. I believe I have been called to build just as surely as preachers have been called to preach. God gives us all special talents and my talent happens to be in the construction business. So was my Uncle's. I have done a lot of building during the last thirty years, been involved in projects costing millions of dollars, but I don't think I have yet topped Uncle Emmett's kissing bridge. Its value was beyond price.

A few years ago Lowell Thomas wrote a book titled *Seven Wonders of the World*, but he was writing about the ancient world. Any book about the wonders of the modern world would have to include Uncle Emmett's kissing bridge.

He didn't have slide rules, mathematical tables, computers and other devices that bridge builders have today, but he did have the more important requirements for success—God-given natural ability, the right attitude toward the task, determination, faith, energy and disciplined boldness.

Yes, when a friend tells me how a song, a poem, a painting influenced his life, I think of Uncle Emmett's kissing bridge—and nod knowingly.

3

A LUCKY KID

Let me tell you more about my childhood, the environment in which I started life. I enjoy going back home in memory. I find it pleasant to lean back in my chair, close my eyes and become a kid again for a few minutes. It's better than a coffee break, and it can be a profitable diversion, too. Sometimes, by looking at the way the little Wallace twig was bent years ago, I can better understand why the Johnson tree leans the way it does today.

As I have already mentioned, I was born in Edinburg, Leake County, which is in east-central Mississippi. It was a little country town of several hundred population. It has grown since then and now has about a thousand people.

Edinburg wasn't on a railroad, and a town that wasn't on a railroad in those days was regarded as a hick place by sophisticated folks. We were what was known as "country jakes." Still, I think I got off to as lucky a start in life as a boy could have. But don't misunderstand me. I don't mean that my parents were well fixed and I had so-called advantages. Not at all. In fact, children born today in the same kind of economic environment into which I was born are considered underprivileged and are the objects of great concern by charity, benevolent and governmental agencies. A war on poverty is being fought with their rescue as its goal. How times change!

I was born October 5, 1901, in a little rented farmhouse, to Alva and Josephine Johnson. That was both a good and a bad time to be born. October is a glorious month in Mississippi. The sun shines, the air is cool and invigorating, the leaves are beginning to turn red, yellow and gold, and the cotton bolls are exploding into beautiful puffs of white. It's harvest time, pickers are in the fields, the gins are humming, people have money and the merchants are smiling.

So, looking at it from one standpoint, October is a mighty good month in which to be born. The weather is right and folks are in a good humor.

But looking at it from another standpoint, October wasn't such a good month for arriving—not in those days. Everybody was busy, and the menfolks didn't like to see the women folks take time out to have babies. They were needed in the kitchen to cook and feed hungry husbands and hands, and women also sometimes helped out in the fields. When cotton is ready to be picked, it has to be picked. Let bad weather catch it in the field, and its quality is damaged.

Although I didn't select the most convenient time to be born, my parents gave me a grand welcome. I, of course, don't remember anything about my life during those first days, but my father and mother told me many times in later years how happy my birth had made them. What's more, they showed their love in so many ways. My father died some years ago, but my mother lived to be ninety-six.

She was pert, interested in life, and continued to paint pictures to the end!

I was the first grandchild for my mother's parents, the Edwardses, and the first for my father's parents. So you can imagine what a to-do they made over me.

Tragedy struck soon after I was born. My mother became ill with typhoid fever and was sick for six weeks. When the doctor told her they would have to take me, the baby, away from her, she protested vigorously. But she consented when she became convinced that it was for my own protection. I was moved to a room across the hall, but our old family doctor said it would be all right for me to be taken to my mother for a very brief period twice a day. I doubt that a modern doctor would permit such a practice.

Mother was critically ill, and for a while it was thought that she wouldn't live. She herself, however, never entertained any thought of dying. She was a little woman who weighed only about a hundred pounds, but she always had plenty of spunk and determination—and faith in God. Because of her faith and courage, she never doubted she would recover and never worried too much. She had the right attitude.

Mother, being so little, was in striking contrast to my father. He was a huge man—six feet and six inches tall, broad shoulders, lean, with the arms of a blacksmith, which he was. He also was a carpenter, mechanic, farmer. You name it, and Dad could do it. All the Johnsons were like that. Some of my paternal ancestors also were Presbyterian preachers.

Anyway, little Mother and big Father made an interesting couple.

Mother's people, by the way, were school teachers, artists, bookkeepers, workers at the quiet and more sedentary pursuits.

So I think I am fortunate to come from a mixture of two such backgrounds.

There are other factors which convince me that I got off to a very fortunate start in life and for which I am thankful. Although my parents were poor tenant farmers at the time I was born, they were devout Christians, rugged, hard-working, honest people of character. They had pride and self-respect and would have been insulted by any offer of charity. They wanted to work for what they got—and did.

Although we were poor economically, I don't think anyone looked down on us. Both my mother and father belonged to old Mississippi families. I remember some of the thrilling stories my Grandmother Edwards told me. She and her family had come into Edinburg by boat on Pearl River and settled there. The closest family to them was five or six miles away. It was lonely, wild country.

One day Grandma was going to visit neighbors, riding a horse sidesaddle. She said that all of a sudden her horse stopped and she nearly fell off. Standing in the road just ahead of her was a panther, crouched and staring as if he were ready to spring. She wondered what in the world was going to happen. But she didn't freeze in horror. Grandma Edwards said she let out the wildest scream ever heard in that part of Mississippi, and it nearly scared the daylights out of the panther. He went scooting into the woods.

Rangers in our national parks say that one of the best defenses against attacking animals is a lot of yelling, screaming and loud noise. But nobody ever had to tell Grandma Edwards that. It was just automatic with her. Her little grandson Wallace also was known to use the tactic in situations involving advancing parents instead of panthers, but not always with her success.

Our family roots went back to pioneer days. And although there near Edinburg we lived in a rented cottage, we were only two miles from the stately old home that had been built by Great-grandfather Johnson Monroe Hooper in 1840, and some of its dignity and prestige were reflected on us poor Johnsons.

My mother's people traced their ancestry back to Jonathan Edwards, the famous New England educator, theologian and missionary to the Indians.

Yes, we were "well connected," as people used to say, on both sides of the family, with a Confederate background. No one looked down their noses at us because of our poverty. During the terrible Reconstruction period following the Civil War, poverty was common even among the oldest and most aristocratic families. In fact, poverty in those days was almost a status symbol. It took years for many families to recover financially, and some never did.

But, you know, even adversity frequently has its compensations. The hardships of those Reconstruction days drew people close together in a spirit of neighborliness that seems to be lacking today.

But now let's get back to my mother's illness soon after my birth. Her condition was so critical that several doctors were called in. They were kind and dedicated old gentlemen, but in the light of modern knowledge and techniques they were ignorant about many diseases. But Mother survived both the typhoid fever and the treatment, and she came out of the experience an even stronger Christian.

She has told me how she used a rocking chair for a cradle. Every morning after she fed and bathed me she rocked me to sleep and then placed me on a feather pillow in the chair. She would fasten me in so I couldn't fall and would put sticks of stove wood under the rockers so they couldn't rock. Then, before starting her housework, she would kneel beside the rocker and thank God for her many blessings, ask that His guiding hand rest upon her and my father and me throughout the day, and would pray that her boy would grow up to lead a useful life. Then she went about her tasks in a happy, confident frame of mind. She was ready to cope with whatever the day brought.

See what I mean when I say I got off to a most fortunate start in life?

Mother and Father didn't know anything about babysitters. When they went to church, they bundled me up and took me with them.

One night when I was eight months old they returned home from a revival. Mother got out of the buggy in front of the house and went in, carrying me, and Dad drove on to the barn.

When he came into the house, he told my mother that he wanted her to kneel with him beside my bed. "I want us to rededicate our lives to God," he said, "and I want us also to dedicate our son to God's service." And they knelt and prayed. I wasn't consulted about my dedication, of course, but I have never had reason to object to it nor to doubt that God heard their prayers. I have carried that picture of my mother and father, kneeling in dedicatory prayer, in my mind and heart all through life. It has helped me in many a difficulty, in many a trying moment.

It would be hard to get away from an influence like that even if I wanted to, which I don't.

Underprivileged child? I was a most privileged child to live in a home like that, out in the beauty, peace and freedom of the country.

We were a rich family—just a little short of cash.

4

FAMILY ON THE MOVE

Although my parents were making a living as sharecroppers there on the farm near Edinburg, with Dad adding to the income by doing odd jobs as a mechanic and carpenter, they became dissatisfied. What money they had saved toward the possible purchase of a little farm in the area had been wiped out by Mother's illness. So they began to pray for God to open up something better—to direct them to a place where there was more opportunity, especially for little Wallace. They were ambitious for their son to go to a good school, to grow up in an environment that would give him a better chance to succeed in life.

Mother loves to tell the story. They soon got an answer to their prayers—almost a miraculous answer, in her opinion.

One Sunday afternoon a man named Aaron Pace, and a younger man whose name I don't recall, came to see Dad. Mr. Pace said he was buying a place two or three miles out from Kosciusko and there was another small farm for sale right near it. He suggested that Dad go up there with him and look at it on Thursday. He wanted Dad to buy it and be his neighbor.

Well, Dad said he'd like to have a place of his own, but, goodness, he didn't have any money. Wouldn't do much good to go and look at it.

The men were sitting on the porch talking. Mother was sitting just inside the door. She wasn't exactly eavesdropping, but she caught a few words of the conversation— enough to get the drift of it. She became aware that Mr. Pace was trying to talk Dad into moving up near Kosciusko, and from then on she was all ears. Kosciusko was the seat of the adjoining county, Attala. It was on a railroad and had a good school and was a town with a lot of promise. A move up there seemed to be exactly what Mother had been praying for. Her hopes soared. But they had a very short flight, for in a moment or two she saw Dad shaking his head and heard him saying, well, he had cotton to pick and other things to do and hardly thought he could get away. Fear gripped her. Opportunity was knocking, and Dad was about to slam the door in its face. She knew she had to do something and do it fast.

Mother stepped out on the porch, trying to look casual but all trembly inside. She spoke pleasantly to the visitors and said she couldn't help but hear a part of their conversation. And then, smiling at Mr. Pace, she said, "Yes, Al can go with you." Then she looked at Dad and said, "You and your brother can get in the rest of the cotton between now and Thursday, and you don't have to worry about the baby and me. We'll look after everything and will get along just fine."

Dad, as I have pointed out, didn't have any money and still didn't see much sense in going 'way up there to look at a farm he couldn't buy. It was twenty-five miles one way, and that was a long buggy trip. But Mother had put him on the spot, and she seemed so excited by the prospect that he told Mr. Pace he'd go.

The two farms for sale were in the Williamsville community out from Kosciusko. I don't think you will find it on a map today.

Well, Dad liked the farm near the one Mr. Pace bought. To own a place would open up a fresh start for him and Mother and their baby son. He came back interested but somewhat depressed. He just didn't have the money—not even enough to make a down payment. They prayed over the matter.

Then Mother remembered something. Maybe it was the answer. She recalled that Dr. Newt Stuart, who had delivered me when I was born had said to Dad, "Al, if I can ever help you in any way, let me know." She knew he really meant it, and she talked Dad into going to see him and asking for a loan. So Dad did, and he got it. I think it was three hundred dollars, or maybe it was three hundred and fifty. That was a lot of money in those days. That completed the answer to Mother's prayer. She and Dad weren't exactly marching to Zion, but they were on their way to a land of greater opportunity. I was then about two years old.

Dad built a small house on the farm, and we moved in. It was December, with lots of cold rain and mud. We were more or less marooned with a meager supply of groceries. Nobody came to see us except Mr. Pace and his family. They hiked through the woods to our place. We didn't have a gay Christmas that year, but we had a happy one. We were on our own place, ready to make our own crop, come spring. And down there spring comes in March. When the weather got pleasant and the buds began to swell and the birds started singing, other people, some of them leaders of

the community, came to see us, to welcome us to Williamsville. Mother tells me that four large families came at one
time. They sat in chairs, on beds, on the floor, just filled the
whole house. We didn't feel alone anymore. We had found
wonderful new friends. Mother and Dad took part in church
and neighborhood activities and became a real part of the
life there.

When I was four years old my aunts gave me a little tool
chest for Christmas—a little hammer, saw, square, chisel
and some nails. It was the most thrilling thing I had ever
had, and I really gave Mother a workout from then on. I
went around sawing, driving nails, the busiest young carpenter in Mississippi. My interest in hammering and sawing, trying to make things, was no mere passing childish
fancy, whipped up by new toys. It continued. Mother tells
me that I even sometimes bought nails with nickels they
had given me for candy.

On February 11, 1905, a big event happened. There was
some excitement around the house, the doctor came, neighbor women dropped by, and I was sent out to build something. And soon Dad told me some wonderful news. I had
a baby brother. His name was Alva Graves.

The new baby became the center of attraction, but I
don't recall that I was neglected, and I don't recall that I
was jealous. I was happy at the thought of having a little
brother to play with.

Grandpa and Grandma Edwards moved up to Williamsville about that time. Dad sold them a part of our farm, and
they built a home near us. It was good to have them living
near, and we had happy times together. Mother made my
clothes, and she soon learned that she had better not forget
to put a patch hip pocket on my knee pants—or britches,
as we called them. If she got in a hurry and neglected to do
that, she got an awful howl out of me. I had to have that

pocket. I always put an envelope in it—one that would stick up high and be seen easily. That showed I was a businessman, a big shot. Sometimes I also carried my hammer in that back pocket, and I usually had a pencil about my ear. I used it to mark boards that I would saw and when I got paper and pretended to be figuring or writing.

I guess I was a little ham, all right, but I like to think that even as a five-year-old kid I somehow realized that it pays to advertise, to attract attention in a constructive way, to put up a good rear as well as a good front.

When I was about six I received another present that thrilled me and created more strain for my parents. Uncle Emmett, our famous bridge builder whom I already have told you about, gave me a little ax. Although it was small, it was the real thing.

I quit being a carpenter and became a lumberjack. I guess Mother and Dad had to keep a pretty close watch on me, to protect the house and furniture, and also to keep me from chopping off my foot. One day I got ambitious. There was a small gum tree in back of the house, and I asked Mother if I might chop it down. George Washington is said to have chopped down a cherry tree without first obtaining permission and got into trouble, and I wasn't going to make that mistake. Mother said yes, it would be O.K. for me to cut it down. She thought I would hack on it awhile and then move on to something else. But I didn't. I stayed with it. I whacked and whacked and rested and whacked some more.

I didn't get the job finished that day, but I went back to it the next morning. And I finally cut down the gum tree. I don't suppose it was more than five or six inches in diameter, but it looked as large to me then as a giant redwood. I was pretty proud of myself—and Mother tells me she and Dad were a little proud of me, too, for sticking to the job.

After that, I combined lumberjacking and carpentering

and stuffed more envelopes in my britches pocket and kept busy. Even as a small boy, I enjoyed "working" more than playing childish games.

My little work projects kept me out in the yard, out in the fresh air, and I sometimes became very impatient when something interfered with them.

One day Mother called me into the bedroom and told me to keep an eye on my little brother Graves. She had to go to the kitchen to attend to some cooking. I had something I wanted to do, and I sat there squirming and fretting. It seemed that Mother never would come back and relieve me. So I thought up what struck me as a brilliant piece of strategy. I slapped Graves, and, of course, he let out a mighty howl.

Mother heard him and came running to see what had happened. "What's the matter with him?" she asked.

And I told her the truth. "I slapped him," I said.

She looked at me in astonishment. "What for?" she asked.

I said I slapped him to make her come on back. I was tired of watching him. I wanted to go out in the yard.

"Well," she said, "I'll just give your slap right back to you." And she let me have it.

I deserved it, of course, and I'm glad to this day that she did let me have it. As I have thought about the incident in later years, I have learned a lesson from it—the importance of thinking a piece of strategy all the way through, if possible, before you start. My idea for making Mother come back to the baby was sure-fire, but I hadn't given any thought to what would happen after she got there.

Sometimes from the small, relatively unimportant incidents of life—and often in childhood—we learn more truths than we learn from the big events.

Along about that time Uncle Emmett moved to a little place out from Hattiesburg, Mississippi, and went to work for a sawmill. He induced us to sell out and move down there, too. The sawmill would give Dad a job, and the certainty of a weekly pay check beat the uncertainty of farming.

Things didn't turn out so well. That was in 1907, and a depression set in, only they called it a panic. Old-timers still talk of the panic of 1907. Jobs soon became scarce, there was little market for lumber, nobody had any money, and businesses went on the rocks. When the sawmill operated, they paid off in script that was good only at their commissary. Times were awfully hard.

Dad decided to move back northward to the old home territory. Farmers didn't have any money, but they were still eating pretty well. He'd try farming again.

We moved to a farm owned by Bill Mayo near Carthage, Mississippi. Mr. Mayo had married one of Mother's sisters.

Between our farm and the adjoining farm there was a creek. We had a very rainy spring, and the creek flooded and spread out over the fields. We were marooned for several days and almost ran completely out of food.

Graves and I had the usual childhood diseases. Once when we were coughing badly, Mother had the doctor to take a look at us. He said we had whooping cough. Among the remedies he prescribed was castor oil.

That scared me, for I had taken the stuff before and knew how awful it was. In those days castor oil was a pretty common remedy for whatever ailed a child. So after the doctor left and before Mother could get around to dosing us, I stole the castor-oil bottle, slipped out and hid it under the house.

When Mother was ready to give us the medicine, she, of course, couldn't find the castor oil. She knew she had some, and she knew where it was supposed to be. I must have had a very guilty look, for she soon suspected me. She grilled me, and her attitude and tone were such that I decided I had better come clean. She didn't whip me for doing such a sneaky thing—maybe she feared a licking would bring on a bad spell of coughing—but it did seem that she gave me an unnecessarily large dose.

That fall I quit being a carpenter and lumberjack and became a cotton-picker. I was about seven years old—hadn't yet started to school—and I said I was going to pick a bale of cotton. I picked every day when the weather wasn't bad, and I kept at it. I'd pick fifteen or twenty pounds at a time. I was picking our own crop, so I wasn't doing it for money. I just wanted to work. It was fun to have a goal and struggle toward it.

I finished my bale before the fall was over. It takes about fourteen hundred pounds of seed cotton to gin out a bale of lint weighing about five hundred pounds.

We lived there on Mr. Mayo's farm near Carthage for about a year, and then we moved back to Williamsville. Dad decided to try something else. He built a little shop and became a blacksmith.

Spurred on by my triumph in picking a bale of cotton, I decided I wanted to be a farmer, not just a field hand. I wanted to plow and make a crop. A neighbor who had time to encourage an ambitious youngster said he'd teach me to plow, and he did. And I stuck to my ambition to make a crop. I plowed and worked a small corn patch and made thirty-five or forty bushels, with just a little help.

While I was working in the field, many other boys my age were fishing and swimming, playing ball or hunting. I would join the fun occasionally, but I had a much better time working.

I never enjoyed hunting. Somebody gave me a rifle when I got older—maybe eleven or twelve—but I used it only a few times. I didn't like to kill birds and animals.

5

GROWING UP

It was after we moved back to Williamsville that I started to school for the first time. My teacher was Aunt Georgia, one of Mother's sisters. At that time the community did not have a regular schoolhouse, and classes were held in a little church.

I don't suppose any boy ever got off to a worse start in school than I did. I didn't know you could hold your hand up and be excused when you had to go to the little house out behind the church. I hadn't been in class very long that first day when I began to get uncomfortable. I guess the excitement and strain of starting to school was just a little too much. So, after a while I began to squirm and suffer. Finally, I was just about to pop and couldn't hold out any longer. Quite an embarrassing commotion followed.

You can be sure my poor, flustered aunt got me aside and explained how I was to handle such urges in the future.

The only thing I liked about school was recess. I didn't

feel that I needed to go to school. Why, hadn't I picked a bale of cotton? I was ready to go to work at a regular job.

Having my aunt as teacher had some advantages and some disadvantages. The other children often accused me of being teacher's pet, and their teasing sometimes would lead to fights. One day I had a fight with Frank Winters and came out second. I ran into the schoolroom crying. When Aunt Georgia asked me what was the matter, I said Frank hit me with a biscuit. She thought I said, "with a big stick," and she went after Frank. She was angry, and it took some fast explaining to save Frank from the worst thrashing of his life.

Some of those cold, hard biscuits brought to school for lunch by my classmates were pretty wicked things when used as missiles. I think I'd have just as well been hit with a big stick as with one of those biscuits.

Aunt Georgia had a tendency to favor me, to spoil me, I suppose, and I may have taken advantage of that. She was an excellent teacher, but, as a rule, I don't think it is a good idea for a child to be taught by his aunt and it was probably best I had her for only one year.

I went through the fifth grade at the little Williamsville school, and, for higher learning, Dad and Mother decided I should go to school in Kosciusko. Dad bought me a little horse to ride to the town school every day. His name was Sammy. Five or six other kids in our community also rode horses to the Kosciusko school. The distance was three or four miles.

We had to cross a long wooden bridge over a creek and the bottoms—it seemed a mile long—and I don't see why every one of us, including the horses, wasn't killed. We used to race across that rattling bridge as fast as our horses could run. I'll never understand why we didn't knock holes in the floor.

Those daily races, both going to and coming from school, always ended in humiliation for me. Sammy was just too small to compete with the other boys' and girls' larger horses. He did the best he could, but we always brought up the tail end, eating their dust and listening to their giggles and guffaws. What made losing even more embarrassing was the fact that Sammy and I made a ridiculous spectacle —me, a big overgrown boy bouncing on such a little horse, with my long legs dangling almost to the ground and my arms flailing the air as I tried to urge my runty mount on to greater speed. I am sure there were times when it looked as if little Sammy should have been riding me instead of vice versa.

I think my experiences gave me an attitude of defeatism toward nearly everything. I reached the point where I didn't want to go to school anymore and suffer the daily humiliation. Finally, I rebelled. I said, "Dad, I don't wanta go. I will not go back. I am not going to keep on being the tail end every day."

They made me finish the term, but I failed. That meant I'd have to take the sixth grade over again the next year. I was nearly in tears at the thought of riding Sammy another year.

But Dad and Mother were understanding parents and knew how I felt and decided to do something about it. So, when I was ready to go back to school for the new term, Dad bought me a larger and faster horse, Bob, and a brand-new bridle and saddle. Bob was a real going Jesse. He could outrun everything.

From then on I didn't suffer any more humiliation. Instead of being the tail end of the race across the long bridge every day, Bob and I became the head end. That restored my confidence and self-respect, and it had a transforming effect on my school work. I lived in a new and happy world.

Dad added a grist mill to his blacksmith shop about that time and did right well. He did so well, in fact, that he bought the first Ford car in the county, and I was determined to learn to drive it. Everybody was afraid of it, including the horses and cows.

I'll never forget one Sunday night when we went to church in it. We were Baptists. We went early and parked close to the church. Dad said that after church we'd hold back and wait till everybody got safely away in their buggies and on their horses before we cranked up. We didn't want to frighten any horses and cause them to run away.

We had those old presto-carbon lights on the Ford. You had to turn water on to make gas to burn in them. I slipped out before church service was over and went to light our lights. I'd have everything ready when my folks came out. Well, something went wrong with the lights, and while I was fiddling around trying to fix them, the car burst into flames!

A lot of excitement followed, naturally. People came boiling out of the church. Horses ran away, and their owners took out after them, shouting, "Whoa! Whoa!" Women screamed, "Keep away from that car." We finally put out the fire, but the Johnsons were a mighty unpopular family that night.

And I imagine a good bit of conversation centered on the advantages of horse and buggy over car as families made their way behind Ole Dobbin.

That was an interesting little church. One Sunday it was a Baptist church, the next Sunday a Methodist, and then a Presbyterian. Congregations took turns holding services there.

It was in that little country church that I accepted Jesus Christ as my Lord and Savior.

That was during a revival conducted by the Reverend

W. A. Roper, pastor of the Baptist church in Kosciusko. No pressure had been put on me. No tearful pleading. I was not in an emotional state, and I was not acting impulsively. I had been thinking about making a public profession of what I felt in my heart and had told my parents that I was going to do it and join the church. They approved and were glad.

So when Brother Roper gave the invitation that Sunday night, I went down the aisle all by myself and accepted Jesus and gave my heart to God. I felt that my sins had been forgiven and that God would take charge of my life and help me to grow up to be the kind of man I should be.

I was eleven, and I had made one of the biggest decisions of my life. I was baptized in nearby Yockanookany Creek, along with others who had made professions at the revival. It was fall and the water was pretty cool, but I felt very warm inside.

Reverend J. A. Ousley, who liked to work with boys, gave me a Bible as a birthday present and marked a passage for my special attention—the second letter of Paul the Apostle to Timothy, 2:15. It reads: "Study to show thyself approved unto God, a workman that needeth not to be ashamed, rightly dividing the word of truth."

That made a deep impression on me. It stuck in my mind and influenced me all through my formative years and on into manhood. I don't think a day goes by that I don't think of that passage, and I quote it often in speeches and conferences. I know of no better advice to give a builder, a businessman, a carpenter, a plumber, a salesman, a banker—anybody. "Study to show thyself approved unto God, a workman that needeth not to be ashamed." I try to measure all my decisions, my actions, against that yardstick.

As I read my Bible, I found many other passages that

impressed me profoundly and which have continued to serve as guidelines for my life. The passages that influenced me the most, next to the one I have just quoted, are Matthew 7:7–8. "Ask, and it shall be given you; seek, and ye shall find; knock, and it shall be opened unto you; For every one that asketh receiveth; and he that seeketh findeth; and to him that knocketh, it shall be opened."

I carry that promise of God in my billfold, written on a little card. I don't really need to have it on a card, as it is written in my mind and heart. But in recommending God and prayer to others who tell me of their problems, I find it helpful to pull out my card and let them read what I so firmly believe and what I have found to be so true.

Getting back to my religious life as a youth: one Sunday when I was about thirteen, I decided that I just didn't want to go to Sunday school. I had been going regularly and enjoying it, and I don't know what had got into me. So I told Mother I wasn't going.

"Wallace," she said softly, "come on and go as usual. If you are tired of going to Sunday school, we can talk about it later. You won't have to go next Sunday if you don't want to, but you must go this Sunday."

I went, and in the class that morning I met a redheaded boy named Calton Edwards, a newcomer from Ackerman. We became friends at once, and that was the beginning of a wonderful friendship that grew and continued a long time and meant much to me. As Mother pointed out, if I had stayed home that morning I wouldn't have met Calton. I don't think I had ever objected to going to Sunday school before that, and I don't think I ever have since then.

When I was about thirteen, I had another experience that remains in my memory as one of the most exciting and happiest days of my life. That was the day I worked at a regular job and made money. I had worked steadily before that, picking cotton, raising corn, cutting grass, making things, as I have related, but I wasn't working for pay. I was helping my dad, helping to provide for the family. I was working for fun. But this job I want to tell you about was different.

That was a political year, and a big county-wide rally and picnic was held near our place in Williamsville. A grocer set up a refreshment stand and offered me a job helping him. I grabbed it. I was thrilled over the idea of having a regular for-pay job. We had a busy day. I even waited on customers! I sold soft drinks, candy, cookies, chewing gum. I was so busy and excited I wouldn't stop to eat my lunch, and I went home tired and proud, jingling my pay. I have forgotten how much I made, but I know it seemed to be a tremendous sum.

Anyway, about the time I finished the seventh grade, Dad got restless again. He was always looking for greener pastures. He decided to sell his blacksmith shop and grist mill at Williamsville and move to Texas. He had heard reports of great opportunities out there. So he got on the train and went to investigate.

He came back full of enthusiasm. He had found a tract he could lease near Beaumont. I don't know exactly what he had in mind to do in Texas, whether he wanted to be a rancher or continue to be a blacksmith. Maybe he was going to do both. He got busy making preparations to move us. He bought some horses and mules and tried to interest others in moving to Texas. We'd form a caravan and go in wagons and buggies, a sort of covered-wagon expedition.

But Texas seemed almost like a foreign country to Mother, and she and the rest of our folks were against any such business. You might think that the adventure of it would beckon to a young boy, but it didn't appeal to me, either. I had never had any desire to be a cowboy out West, nor a desire to fight Indians. Now that I think about it, maybe I wasn't a normal kid. I don't recall ever going through the usual robber or soldier stages. My only approach to normality was the time I decided I wanted to be a locomotive engineer as my Grandfather Johnson had been. It was a boast in the family that, as a young railroader, he had been the engineer to pull the first train into Mississippi. So one day when I heard him tell of his exciting experiences, I said I, too, wanted to be an engineer. But he said, "No, Wallace. Take my advice. Don't be an engineer. It's too dangerous. The life of the average engineer is only seven years." I gave up that ambition right quick.

Well, as I said, all the family were against Dad's moving to Texas. I didn't want to be a cowboy. I had seen Uncle Emmett's famous kissing bridge, and I was going to be a carpenter, a builder, and I could be that right there in Mississippi, at home. We put the pressure on Dad and talked him out of it.

6

OUR HAPPIEST MOVE

Instead of moving to faraway Texas, we moved to Zama, Mississippi, a new and pretty little town only about eighteen miles away from Williamsville. It was the luckiest and happiest of Dad's many moves, as far as I was concerned. It was at Zama that I met a beautiful girl named Alma McCool, who later was to become my wife.

Dad became the blacksmith for the sawmill at Zama, and we moved into a new house built on the side of a hill. You talk about these modern split-level homes? Huh! We had a real split-level at Zama, including a porch about thirty feet from the ground.

Soon a family moved into a house on the next street, a house that backed up to ours, with a dip in the back lots. They were the McCools—Mr. and Mrs. Ernest McCool, their pretty daughter Alma and their son Bernard, but known as Barney. Mr. and Mrs. McCool had had other children, but Alma and Barney were the only ones who had survived.

I was older than Alma and Barney. They were nearer the age of my brother Graves. Besides, I was older than my years, because I was always working at jobs usually held by older boys and young adults. So I didn't play with Alma and Barney very much. They played with Graves more. I didn't run around much socially—didn't go to many dances or parties—but when I did it was with an older bunch. But I did play with Alma, Barney and Graves some, and when there was a snow one time I did help build a sled and joined in the fun of sliding down the hill. And I certainly took notice of how pretty Alma was and what fun she was to be with.

We were in the same grade in the Zama school and walked to school together often. Romance was soon buzzing in my head and making my heart beat a little faster when she smiled at me.

Grandpa Johnson was selling machinery in those days, and he sold a shingle mill to the people who were developing Zama. My brother and I got a job stacking the shingles in bundles at the mill. They were made of cypress, and I didn't know till then that so much sand can get into the grain of cypress wood. After handling those shingles for several hours, my fingers would be bleeding, cut by the sand.

It was while working there that I talked Mr. Howell, the manager, into giving me a job as a carpenter. I assured him I could do the work, and he said he'd let me have a try at it. I built myself a nice tool box, and then I took some of my shingle money and bought tools—a hammer, several saws, chisels, planers, a square, a jointer, screwdrivers, a brace and a set of bits. Oh, I had everything that a full-fledged carpenter would have. I had learned something, you see. I had learned that if a carpenter had a good box of tools, why, that was the yardstick by which employers measured his ability. It helped to determine the amount of his pay. So I bought all the tools I could afford. I didn't know how to use all of them, but I put up a good front and went to work at $1.25 an hour.

I was sixteen years old when I picked up my well-filled tool box and went to work as a carpenter—and I felt I was thirty. Why, wasn't I doing a man's work and making a man's pay? I looked down on boys my age. Girls my age were another matter. I still had eyes for that pretty little Alma. I felt that when she got a little older she could make tracks around my flour barrel any time she wanted to. She was as pretty as a speckled pup on a banana wagon.

All of us worked, and we got along rather well there in Zama. We had a cow, as many people did in those days, and that cow, indirectly, almost cost me my life. Graves and I took turns in driving her up to the house from the pasture for milking. Well, I had the flu, and one day soon after I got out again I went to get the cow. She was stubborn and didn't want to go home, and I became completely exhausted running after her. When I got home, I had to go to bed. Dr. Turnage, who lived across the street, was called, and he said I had double pneumonia.

That was the second time I had it, and once more my condition became so critical that my family almost gave up hope for my recovery. But they kept praying, and Dr. Turnage, bless his heart, kept working with me. He stayed at my bedside the whole of one day and all night.

One day, Mother, who was so concerned over my illness that she was almost ill herself, said to the doctor, "Dr. Turnage, don't you let my boy die."

"Mrs. Johnson," he replied, "Wallace is in God's hands. We are merely instruments. We do the best we can, but we don't always know whether the things we do are best or not. You just keep on praying."

So Mother, Dad and Graves kept on praying and the doctor and everybody kept on doing for me. I finally passed through the crisis, and the fever left me. That morning Graves was sent hurrying to the commissary to get some oatmeal and oranges. The doctor wanted me to eat. I had to build up strength. When Graves came back, Dr. Turnage said he wanted the oatmeal cooked several hours. No instant oatmeal in those days.

I had sweated so much as the fever left me that the bed was sopping wet. The bed linens were changed, and I ate my oatmeal and drank orange juice. The doctor said I was going to get well, and left.

Mother, Dad and Graves sat on the bed beside me, and we all started to cry. We were that relieved and thankful.

That was in 1918, and World War I was on. I wasn't old enough for the draft, so I went back to carpentering. Workmen were needed, and I made $1.50 an hour. That was tremendous pay for a seventeen-year-old boy. I quit school. But I didn't quit studying. I got a copy of *Radford's Estimator*, the book that had been such a help to Uncle Emmett in building his kissing bridge. During my spare time I'd sit down with my handbook and try to learn how to figure construction jobs, learn about design and the strength of materials, how to make blueprints and read them—and all that sort of thing. I knew what I wanted to be, and I was hungry to learn all I could in preparation for it.

Once more Dad got restless, ambitious to move on over the horizon to better fortune. He had heard how amazingly fertile the land was over in the Mississippi Delta. You could grow a bale of cotton to the acre without even trying. Put out a little effort and you'd get two bales to the acre.

Dad talked with our neighbors, the McCools, and got them worked up over the thought of getting rich in the Delta.

So we all moved in 1918. The McCools went to a place near Indianola, and we Johnsons moved to a farm at Helms, eight miles north of Leland. We became sharecroppers and raised cotton. It was selling for a dollar a pound, and everybody said it would go to $1.50. The war was still on.

We had to sell some of our crop to get money to live on, but we held all we could, looking toward higher prices. We played it wrong, though. After the war ended, the bottom dropped out of the market. I think we got thirty cents a pound for the cotton we had refused to sell at a dollar.

But that was a minor tragedy compared to the big one that came to us at Helms. My brother Graves became ill with malaria. His condition kept getting worse, and I remember getting up at two o'clock one morning and running up the road to get the doctor. He came but arrived too late. Graves was dead.

We went back to the old home territory near Kosciusko for the funeral. He was buried in the cemetery where some of Mother's people were buried. He was fifteen years old when he died.

His death was a terrible blow to Mother, Dad and me. We were a closely knit family. It was hard to become resigned to the fact that he was gone, but our faith in God sustained us. We were comforted, too, by Graves's faith, which had never wavered. Mother says he knew he was going to die, and he knew he was going to his heavenly home. That helped us to carry on during those sad days.

After the misfortune we had had at Helms, we were ready for new scenes, a fresh start. It was time for Dad's pendulum to swing from farming back to blacksmithing. We moved to Moorhead, Mississippi, and he put up a shop. Just as he was getting started, more trouble hit us.

Dad became ill with smallpox. That, of course, was a

dreaded disease, and a case of it would cause fear and excitement to sweep through a community. Our house was quarantined, and Dad was shut up in a room by himself at his own demand. Food was put into his room through the window. But that's the way he wanted it. He was so afraid some of us would catch the disease. I'd sneak up to the window and look in at him and see how he was suffering. I felt so sorry for him. He suffered and sweated through it.

I had kept developing as a carpenter and by that time was a pretty good one. I could put in windows, hang doors, install flooring—do it all. I did some work for a contractor at Sunflower and saved some money. I had lacked two years of finishing high school when I quit, and at times I wondered if I had made a mistake. But the $1.50 an hour I was making kept convincing me that I hadn't. Why go to school when I could make that kind of money?

After Dad got over the smallpox, he, too, started carpentering along with his blacksmithing. We worked together on gins.

I have mentioned that the McCools moved from Zama to a place near Indianola and that the move separated Alma and me. But it didn't stop my interest in courting her. I wrote to her, and I went to see her on weekends. It was about twelve miles from Moorhead to their home, and today, of course, that is nothing. Just a little breeze. But in those days of bad roads it was a pretty long trip. Besides, I didn't have a car. So I'd ride the train to Indianola and take a taxi out to the McCools' place in the country. That night I'd walk back into town, stay at the hotel and catch the early train to Moorhead. And after every visit with Alma I'd come away feeling more than ever that she was the girl for me. In fact, Alma was the only sweetheart I ever had. I had had a few dates with other girls but had not done any serious courting.

Alma's parents, Mr. and Mrs. McCool, were fine people. I shall always be grateful for the part they played in my life. Alma's mother gave me a lot of help and encouragement when I was courting, and I needed it, too, at times. Alma had other admirers, and what chance did I, a big, over-grown school drop-out, have in winning such a beautiful and brilliant girl? But Alma's mother, bless her memory, liked me. As I think back over my courting days, I think I can see that Mrs. McCool wanted Alma to fall in love with me as much as I wanted her to. I had a lot of help.

I could afford those weekend courting trips by train and taxi because I was making pretty good money and was saving a good part of it.

When I had saved $1,800, I began to feel my oats. I was only eighteen, but I was ready to become a contractor, by golly. So I made a contract to build a nice house in Moorhead. I don't remember exactly, but I think it was a $9,000 deal. And I felt like a real big shot.

I put my money in a checking account at the bank, and I got me a big checkbook which I stuck in my hip pocket, and I made it flop as I walked down the street. I have told you how, as a little kid, I liked to have an envelope showing in my britches hip pocket. Well, there I was in Moorhead, considerably grown up, but in some respects still that show-off kid, trying to impress people.

It took me two years to build that house. One thing that slowed me up was an expensive and complicated French marble mantel that the owner of the house had furnished and which I had to install. The thing was a mosaic, a landscape, and came in scores of small parts like the pieces of a jigsaw puzzle. I wrestled with that thing for weeks, trying to get that picture together. I'd get going good and think I had it figured out right at last and then find that I was wrong again.

The owner of the house kept asking that the floor plans be changed to provide little extras, and I'd agree to them without charging him for them.

When I finally finished that house, I was broke. I hadn't made a dime for all my work, had lost my $1,800 and was $400 in debt. What'a disastrous start I had made as a contractor!

Now that I look back on the experience I can see that it wasn't such a misfortune after all. It proved something— that I was a born contractor and builder. If I hadn't been, I would have quit after that fiasco. But it didn't cure me. I still remembered Uncle Emmett and his kissing bridge, and I stuck to my determination. I had met and passed a test.

That financial failure was helpful in other ways, too. It proved I wasn't such a big shot, and it brought me down to size. And it made me think about school again. Perhaps I needed a better foundation for my ambition.

I knew Mother thought I should go back and had been praying that I would. Dad by then had started working for the county, and Mother was taking in a few boarders and was painting some pictures and making artificial flowers and rag dolls. We were getting along, she said. I could live at home and go to school.

But despite the fact that I had been humbled somewhat by my failure as a contractor, I still had pretty big ideas about myself. So one day I said to Mother, "I think you are right. I've decided to go back to school."

That made her very happy. Then I added, "I want to go to Georgia Tech in Atlanta and be an architect." Her smile faded.

"But, son," she said quietly, "you're not ready for college yet. You'll have to finish high school first. Then you can go to college."

Well, that took all the wind out of my sails. Me go back to

high school? Me, a twenty-year-old man, go to school and be in the same class with kids? The suggestion made me angry. I stalked on into my room.

Several days passed, and Mother didn't mention my going back to school. I kept thinking and stewing about it. The more I thought about it, the more I became convinced that she was right. To go back would be embarrassing, and it would take courage, but I began to feel that I would be a coward if I didn't. I talked with Professor J. S. Vandiver, the principal of the Moorhead school, and he advised me to finish high school. He greatly encouraged me to do it and said I'd never regret it.

When I went home I told Mother I had decided to go back to school right there in Moorhead, and she was the happiest woman in town. Dad thought I was doing right, too, and I felt better myself.

I didn't want to be entirely dependent on my parents, so I got a job jerking soda and clerking in a drugstore afternoons and on weekends. I continued to write Alma down at Indianola and went there to court her every chance I got. She was glad I was going to school again, and we both dreamed of being architects and building houses and other things. I'd design the exteriors, and she'd design the interiors.

Going to school with boys fifteen and sixteen years old was awfully embarrassing at times. Not only was I twenty when I started, but I was big and looked a lot older. I was six feet four and weighed over two hundred pounds. They called me big-jointed and double-jointed, old Cornwallace Johnson, Dad, Grandpa, and other things. They'd laugh when I'd make some dumb mistake in class—and I made plenty—and often, in their general attitude, seemed to regard me as some sort of freak or oddball.

I must admit I wasn't a very brilliant student. I wasn't

good in English, history, science, and never could spell. I guess my early schooling hadn't prepared me very well for high school. Then, too, I had been out of school so long that I had gotten away from the swing of it. The going was rough. My redeeming features were a pretty good memory and a head for figures. They are still my strong points, I think.

But I have always tried to see a thing through, once I have started it. I'm not a quitter. I stuck it out, encouraged all the way by Mother, Professor Vandiver and Alma. I finished high school. I was twenty-two.

7

HALLELUJAH!

After I finished high school, and while I was still working in the drugstore, the owner of a lumberyard at Itta Bena, Mississippi, asked me if I'd like to come down and manage it. That sounded good. It meant an assured income. I could ask Alma to marry me. So I did, and she said "Yes." Hallelujah!

We set our wedding day for August 10—that was in 1924—and I didn't let the fact that I didn't have any money bother me. I had nerve and high hopes, so I went across the street to Stevens Drugstore, our competitor, and asked Mr. Stevens if he would lend me eighty-five dollars. I said I wanted it to get married. He seemed surprised that a boy working for his competitor would come to him for a loan, but he let me have it. Maybe it was such a shock that he agreed before his head cleared. I don't remember my own reasoning in the matter—what made me go to our competitor instead of to my own boss. All I know is that it seemed a good idea at the time and that it worked.

I'd like for the record to show that I paid Mr. Stevens back—at five dollars a month.

We ran into difficulty in planning our wedding, though. We wanted to be married in the Baptist church in Indianola, where Alma was a member, with Reverend Harry Martin, the pastor, officiating. But when we checked with him we found he would be away in Europe on that date— August 10.

We talked the situation over and decided we'd transfer the wedding from the church in Indianola to the church in Moorhead where my parents and I were members. But we ran into another snafu: My pastor also would be away at that time, holding a revival elsewhere.

Then we thought we'd better shift the scene back to Indianola, and Mother suggested that we get Brother Ousley to come and officiate. He was then in Tutwiler. He was an old friend of the family—the preacher who had given me a Bible on my tenth birthday.

We got in touch with him. He said he'd be happy to marry us, but he would have to return immediately after the ceremony. He couldn't make train connections if we were married in Indianola, but he could if we were married in Moorhead. So once more we changed our plans, to suit his schedule.

Alma's father and her brother Barney drove over to Moorhead on a Sunday morning, and we were married in the living room of my parents' home. It was a simple, pretty wedding, with just relatives and a few friends present.

We had a good dinner, and then I got into a car and drove to the lumberyard in Itta Bena to feed the mules. I had just started on the job and was anxious to get off to a good start.

I couldn't ask them to let me off to go on a honeymoon so soon after going to work there. Besides, we were broke.

But you don't have to take a long trip to have a wonderful honeymoon, and we started one that is still going on.

We moved into a cute little rented bungalow on the bank of the lake in Itta Bena. It was a nice honeymoon cottage—and, what's more, we had furniture. Alma's mother had died just before Alma finished high school, and since her brother Barney was going off to school, her father decided he would break up housekeeping. He gave us their furniture.

That little bungalow looking out across the lake was a dream place to us. We got off to the happiest kind of start together. We'd get up early, fix breakfast, and then I'd be off to the lumberyard by seven o'clock, full of vim and vigor, ready for another busy and triumphant day. As manager I had to do a lot of everything—buying, selling, seeing that deliveries were made, collecting, bookkeeping, drawing plans for homes and cabins, specifying the materials needed and the cost of the whole job. If a plantation owner came in and asked for a price on ten cabins, for instance, I gave it to him.

I had never managed a lumberyard before, of course, but I had confidence that I could do it. I had studied my *Radford* book well and previously had made blueprints just for the practice. I'd clamp the drawing and the sensitized paper on a board, expose it to sunlight, and then wash it quickly by plunging it into a horse trough. And, of course, my experience as a carpenter was helpful. We worked six long days a week.

My brother-in-law, Barney McCool, who is a partner now with Alma and me in most of our enterprises, came to work for me at the lumberyard during summer vacation while he was going to college. He likes to kid me in front of our associates. He says I was a very unreasonable boss and a terrible slave-driver—that I expected everybody to work as hard as I did.

Barney says that one time I assigned him and a helper to unload a railroad carload of cement, over five hundred bags to be stacked under a shed.

"When you get through unloading the car," he says I told him, "I want you to paint the shed. I'll be back later to tell you what to do the rest of the day."

I think Barney may be exaggerating a little, but I can't say it didn't happen. I know I was having a great time seeing how much I could get done in a day and assumed that everybody else was, too.

Barney also likes to tell how I'd go around the lumberyard acting like a cheerleader, saying, "Hup-hup! Let's turn the world over and see what's on the other side!" And I plead guilty to that. I still like to "Hup-hup!"

If I wasn't too busy I'd go home for dinner. That's what we called lunch, although it was served midday. The evening meal was supper. Alma turned out to be a fine little cook and housekeeper. But, of course, she could have served me boiled sawdust and I would have thought it was delicious. Her housework didn't take all of her time, and she started studying home decoration. She subscribed to magazines dealing with the subject, and she read books about it. The knowledge she gained about interior decoration as a bride was to prove very profitable later when I became a home builder.

We lived for a year in our honeymoon bungalow on the lake in Itta Bena. Then the owners decided they wanted to live in it, and we had to move to another little rented home. We lived there awhile and then bought a small home of our own back on the lake.

That was a big decision—to own our home. It is one of the biggest and most important decisions any couple ever makes. We have emphasized that in our advertising and salesmanship as home builders all through the past quarter of a century. It is sincere advertising, for we speak from our hearts and from our own experience.

As manager of the lumberyard I, of course, had problems and I also had interesting and sometimes amusing experiences. Many of the amusing ones, however, are amusing only in retrospect. Let me tell you of one embarrassing experience.

I tried to keep the yard and our sheds and office as clean and neat as possible. One Saturday morning I was doing some drafting, and I told Frank, one of the Negro employees, to clean up everything—sweep the office, clean off the sidewalk in front of it, straighten up things all around. He was one of our veteran employees, and he was a good one. Frank did a thorough job.

About three o'clock that afternoon I looked out the window and saw a sight that infuriated me. Someone had put new tires on his Ford right in front of our office and had left the old tires and the paper wrappings from the new ones on the sidewalk.

"Frank," I said, "I wish I knew who threw that junk out there. I'd make him eat it."

Frank went to remove the rubbish.

I went on with what I was doing, and in about thirty minutes a giant of a man, about six feet seven inches tall, came stalking in, smelling of Mississippi moonshine. He walked up unsteadily and towered over me.

"I heered that you said that whoever put them old tires and that paper out there, why, if you knowed who did it you would make him eat it," he said, throwing in a lot of profanity.

I got up, and even though I was six feet four I had to look up at him.

"Mister," I said, tapping him on the shoulder, "you needn't mind about eating it. I'll just eat it myself."

I don't list that as one of the big decisions of my life, but I still think it was a pretty wise one.

We had a good, busy, happy life for several years there in Itta Bena and did well till the Depression came in the late 1920s. Then the lumberyard business dwindled away to nothing. Banks started failing, stores closed, the prices of farm products dropped, and there was no hope for improvement soon. The trend was toward even worse conditions.

I put a little job-wanted ad in the Memphis *Commercial Appeal* and got a job as a salesman for a lumber firm in Memphis. I worked hard at it, but against great odds. The Depression kept getting deeper, and it was difficult to make even a small sale. Few people had confidence in the future. Those who had a little money held on to it.

Since I wasn't making any sales, I had a lot of time on my hands, and I didn't waste it. I still clung to my ambition to be a contractor, a builder, in business for myself. So I kept studying handbooks on building, and I drew up plans for houses and estimated their cost, just for practice. I'd draw plans for a home and then see how many ways I could change the basic plan without adding greatly to the cost. I'd work the plan to the left, and then I'd work it to the right.

Finally, I got a chance to take a job as a shipping clerk at a sawmill and lumberyard fourteen miles out from Pine Bluff, Arkansas, at $110 a month, and we left Memphis. It turned out that I was expected to do a lot more than merely ship lumber and keep the records. There wasn't enough shipping to keep a clerk busy, so I had a lot of other duties. I had to do many of the things I had done at Itta Bena, and then some. I had to help run the dry kiln, and at times I had to go out into the woods and select and mark trees for special orders.

The Southern Pine Association lumber inspectors kept me worried and tense a good part of the time. When they came around I was nervous for fear our grades wouldn't hold up. If your sawmill wasn't making good grades, you were in trouble; and if your grades were too high, you were in trouble. If you had too many complaints, you were in trouble; but, on the other hand, if you didn't have any, you were under suspicion. It isn't normal not to have some complaints. I stayed in trouble about half the time, consciously or unconsciously.

The superintendent of the mill was a man from Louisiana, and, like most Louisianians, he loved strong coffee. He'd invite me up to his nearby house to have a cup with him, and, of course, I accepted. I didn't like that strong stuff—sometimes I felt as if I needed someone to lead me after drinking it—but I wanted to be friendly with the boss. We became very close.

Then came a bomb whose explosion knocked Alma and me for a loop, and we still feel a sense of shock when we think about it.

One morning at nine I had coffee with the superintendent at his home. It was a nice coffee break. He was very friendly, as usual, and we chatted about things. Then I went on back to my job at the mill.

About eleven o'clock the superintendent sent a note to our home. Alma read it. It said: "Wallace, upon receipt of this note, you are fired." That's all. No explanation.

Alma got into our Ford and drove to my office at the mill. She came in, crying her heart out, and showed me the note. I was dumfounded. What could it mean? I felt that the world had come to an end. I wasn't making much money, but it was a living. It kept us off the WPA rolls.

My first impulse was to find the superintendent and demand an explanation. But when I went to confront him, I learned he had left the community on a trip and no one knew when he would be back.

I have never seen him since that last morning I had coffee with him on such friendly terms, and I don't know to this day why he fired me. But I do know I am grateful to him, for it turned out to be one of the best things that ever happened to me.

Several years ago I wrote and thanked him, and, as an expression of appreciation, offered him an expense-free vacation at any Holiday Inn. And I wasn't being sarcastic, either. I was sincere. I can't have any ill feeling toward a man who does me a great favor, regardless of whether it was intentional. But he never answered my letter.

But getting back to our predicament when I was fired: We didn't have any savings and I had to have another job in a hurry.

I wrote a little job-wanted ad and sent it to the *Commercial Appeal* in Memphis. I described very briefly my qualifications and experience. But I didn't have my name printed with it. It was a blind ad. The paper was to forward replies to me.

Then I called a friend who was sales manager for Frost Lumber Industries in Little Rock and told him of my situation.

"Wallace, I heard about your being fired, and I'm sorry," he said. "I've been thinking about you, and I've found a job for you at the Barton-Mansfield retail lumberyard in Jonesboro, Arkansas."

That was great news.

We didn't have enough money to hire a truck and take our few pieces of furniture with us. We just packed it up as best we could and stored it. We would have to get it later. That was in 1936.

We went to Jonesboro, and I had worked only one day when I received a letter in answer to the ad I had placed in the Memphis paper. I had notified the paper of my new address. Although the ad hadn't been signed with my name, the man who answered it recognized me from my description of myself. He wrote: "This is in answer to your blind ad. If you are Wallace Johnson who used to work for us in Memphis, report for duty Monday morning."

I showed my new employer the letter. I told him how grateful I was to him for giving me a job, but thought I ought to go on to Memphis. I explained that for years I had been thinking of the day when I could go into the contracting business for myself and felt that I might be able to do that better in Memphis than in Jonesboro. He was understanding and sympathetic.

"Well," he said, "you go on to Memphis and talk with this man. Then if you decide not to accept his offer, you can come on back to us."

We arrived in Memphis on a Saturday night, put our car on the Hotel Chisca parking lot and got a $3.50 room at the hotel. Alma and I had twenty dollars between us. That's all the money we had.

When we got up the next morning, Alma said to me, "Dear, have you got the purse?" I said, "No, I haven't got it."

We became frantic, looking for our purse. We turned nearly everything in that room upside down, but no purse. Alma suggested that maybe we had left it in the car. We were on the sixth floor, but I couldn't wait for the elevator. I went down the stairs, two or three steps at a time. I ran to the parking lot and looked through the car, all trembly and scared. Still no purse.

I went back to the room and made the tragic report to Alma. I had fifteen cents in my pocket, but that wasn't enough for breakfast. We couldn't have eaten anyway, we were so worried.

We finished dressing and went to the car with heavy hearts. I turned a seat down as we were getting in, and the purse fell out! It was one of the most wonderful sights we had ever seen. Oh, what a relief! We were so relieved, and so thankful, that we couldn't talk. We got into the car, tears in our eyes, and didn't say a word till we had driven over a mile out Union Avenue.

We drove on to the home of the man who had offered me the job, but we were so nervous when we got there that we didn't stop. We drove around awhile till we got control of ourselves and then went back to his house. We had a nice visit, and he and his wife invited us to stay for dinner.

"Business is a little better," he said, in discussing the job, "and we want you."

He offered me $37.50 a week as a building-supplies salesman. I decided to take it.

We moved to Memphis once more, and I went to work for the Home Builders Supply Company. They not only sold building materials but built and sold complete houses. I drew plans and specifications for houses, filed the applications, supervised the construction. I used all the information I had learned from *Radford's Estimator* and from my experience, and I learned a lot more as I went along, particularly about loans and finance.

8

A HOUSE A DAY

Alma and I kept dreaming and praying about our ambition to go into business for ourselves. I let my employers know that we were thinking of it, and I promised that I'd never try to take any business from them when we did make the venture. I kept that promise.

Up to that time mortgage bankers had been lending a maximum of 60 percent on the value of a house. So builders required a pretty big down payment from purchasers. As a salesman, I found that kept many people from trying to buy their own home. They just didn't have the down payment. We were coming out of the Depression, but times were still hard.

After the Federal Housing Authority (FHA) came into the home-construction picture, things got better. The FHA started guaranteeing 85 percent of construction costs, and that made it practical for builders to lower the required down payments. That opened a vast field for the construction of low-priced homes.

I felt the time had come to go into business for myself —to take the final step toward our long-dreamed-of goal. That was late in the fall of 1939.

I told my employers of my decision and said I'd stay with them till January 1. They said they hated to see me go but admired my ambition. If I was impatient to get started, it would be O.K. to leave December 1. Perhaps they felt that if I stayed till January 1, I might have conflicting interests during my last month. If so, their fears were unjustified. During the last two weeks that I worked for them I sold six houses, but not once did I suggest to prospective purchasers that if they would wait a little while I might offer them a better bargain. I left them with an inventory of four houses I had planned and built.

So in December, 1939, we went into business on our own, beginning the business that eventually became Wallace E. Johnson Enterprises, Inc. Our first act was to get into our car and drive to the home of Dr. H. P. Hurt, our pastor at Union Avenue Baptist Church in Memphis. We told him we had decided to go into business for ourselves and asked if he would join us in praying to God to bless our venture and direct us all the way. We were moving within His will for us.

I hadn't been able to save any money on my small salary. So it was a bold step we were taking—some called it reckless—but we knew that with God's help we would not fail.

I borrowed two hundred and fifty dollars on our Ford, which was several years old, and agreed to pay it back at twenty-five dollars a month. That was the money we had to live on while we got started building. We had the upstairs apartment of a duplex at 1650 York and paid forty-five dollars a month. The living room became our office.

I went to work designing a five-room house that could

be sold for $2,999. I went to see friends with mortgage companies and told them what I wanted to do, and they were encouraging. I showed my plans to Mr. Buck Horner, head of the FHA in Tennessee, and he also was encouraging.

I arranged to build my first home at 132 South Mc-Kellar Street. I think the street had been named in honor of the late Sen. K. D. McKellar, for years a power in Tennessee politics. That was in January 1940, and I had a rough time getting started with the construction. It was an awfully cold winter. Even the Mississippi River froze over. It took me sixty days to complete the foundation. It was amazing how far we stretched two bits' worth of meat and a nickel's worth of beans. You can do it when you have to, especially if you are doing it for a great purpose.

I finally completed that little house and made $181 on it! I had ended in the black with my second venture as a contractor. I had sold the house before I finished it, so I didn't lose any time starting more houses. I went to see mortgage-banker friends, and they expressed interest and said they would help me.

I figured out twenty-seven different floor plans for my one basic five-room house. That made for economy, and it also helped me avoid monotony in building a lot of homes in the same subdivision.

I was able to get FHA insurance, and I talked a bank into financing me. I also talked building-supplies companies into furnishing me with materials and waiving, or subordinating, to first mortgages. In other words, they said to finance companies: "We have so much faith in Wallace Johnson that we will see that you get your money first and then we will get ours." They waived their lien rights in favor of a first mortgage.

I started ten houses in March 1940, and that was big

front-page news in Memphis, for we weren't completely
out of the Depression. Mike McGee, real-estate editor of
the *Commercial Appeal*, wrote an article about the project.
It was headed: "The Henry Ford of the South Starting 10
Homes at One Time."

It struck him as sensational mass production, even if
the homes were small and were priced at $2,999.

Alma pitched right in with me and was a real partner.
She stayed in the office, which was still a room in our
apartment, answered the phone, kept the books, helped me
with the designing and decorating. I have already told you
how interested she had always been in interior decoration.
This gave her an outlet.

Alma showed me how important interior decoration can
be. She said I must always have one room in a house
painted blue.

"That," she explained, "is for the husband. Most men
like blue. If you let them have just one blue room, they
won't fuss about the others very much, no matter what
color you paint them."

I followed her advice and found she was right. When
we'd show prospective purchasers through a house, the
man might find fault with some features—till we came to
the blue room. After that he would have fewer objections.
He'd just go along with his wife's decisions.

Alma also contributed other good ideas about decora-
tions and conveniences that helped us to sell or rent our
houses. She insisted on plenty of closet space, light, airy
rooms with ventilation. She ordered warm colors for
rooms with northern exposure and cool tints for those on
the south. And before a house was placed on the market,
she checked it for a lot of little things that women might
notice. The screens had to fit snugly, and every speck of
paint had to be removed from window panes, from the

hardware and the floors. Nail heads had to be puttied. Often little things like that can make or break a sale. Never overlook the importance of little things.

I did something that first year in business that is probably the smartest advertising stunt I have ever done. It made us widely known almost overnight. It gave us thousands of dollars' worth of advertising at practically no expense.

I went to a printer and had him print five thousand pasteboard signs. They said: "Let Wallace E. Johnson Build Your Home On This Lot." They cost me half a cent apiece.

The printer said: "Mr. Johnson, the first time these signs get wet, they'll melt and be gone." I said, "Not when I get through with them they won't."

I bought fifty pounds of paraffin and went out into the back yard and heated it in a drum. Then I dipped each of those signs in it. When the wax coating cooled and hardened, they were waterproof.

Well, I put those signs up on vacant lots all over Memphis and Shelby County. I drove all around, sticking up signs here and there. I worked day and night at it.

A few days after I finished, I was at the bank, in line before a teller's window, to make a five-dollar deposit. Also in line was one of the biggest real-estate men in Memphis with a $7,500 deposit. The president of the bank came by and stopped to speak to him. The real-estate man said, "Say, where in God's world did that fellow Wallace E. Johnson come from? He owns more lots than anybody in Memphis." I wanted to laugh but was afraid to. I just kept quiet. The truth of the matter, of course, was that I didn't own any of those lots.

The stunt worked out just fine. Few owners of the lots complained. It was no trouble to remove signs if they objected. Alma was kept busy answering the phone, talking to people who had seen the signs and were interested in having us build houses on lots they especially liked. We'd find out what kind of home they had in mind, and then I'd look up the owner of the lot and get a price on it. With that information in hand, we could give a prospective owner a price on the house and lot.

We got good bargains on the first lots we bought as a result of the sign campaign—very desirable lots for two hundred dollars and three hundred dollars. Often they were lots people had held a long time and were tired of paying taxes on and were ready to unload. But sometimes when we bought only a few lots in an area and built houses on them and later wanted to buy more lots we found that prices had been upped to four hundred dollars or five hundred dollars. We ourselves had increased the price we had to pay.

We soon saw that we just had to do something about our office situation. We had to hire clerical help, and Mr. and Mrs. Paul Harris joined our staff. Our business operations required every bit of space in our upstairs apartment at 1650 York. We'd stand up in the kitchen and eat snacks, and we'd curl up and sleep in a corner. Hundreds of people were coming there and walking up the stairs to our apartment to pick up payroll checks and to transact other business. We were in a residential zone, but our place had become one of the busiest spots in Memphis. But no one complained about the commerical traffic. We shall always be grateful for the patience and forbearance of our neighbors. They had cause for legal action against us and could have made trouble, but they didn't.

But that sort of situation couldn't continue indefinitely. We had to have more space in a suitable location. We prayed about it, and the answer soon came.

Mr. Gordon I. Gordon, an attorney, had the old Lee Lumber Company property for sale on Rayner Street. I took a look at it. The building had been damaged by fire, but the foundation was solid. I made them an offer for the damaged building and fifty by one hundred and fifty feet of ground. I said I would rent the property for ten dollars a month, with an option to buy for three thousand dollars at the end of a year. And if I did buy, the rent money would apply on the purchase price. They accepted the offer.

At the end of the year I had accumulated one hundred and twenty dollars in rent credit toward the purchase and decided to buy. I needed only sixty dollars more for the down payment. I could have bought more ground at the same price at that time but didn't. Later, when we had to have more space, I did buy more, at a price three or four times the original price. But the original deal I made was an excellent one.

We moved our office to 875 Rayner and set up a pre-fabricating plant there which we kept expanding as our business increased through the next few years. We'd cut out whole houses there and rush them to our subdivisions.

The Rayner place remained headquarters for Wallace E. Johnson Enterprises from 1940 till 1968, when we completed construction of a new four-story building on Walnut Grove Road.

We built 181 houses in 1940, a record for one contractor in this area. Some of our building was speculative, which was something new. In other words, we built houses before we had purchasers for them. We built them with the belief that we could sell them.

As the end of 1940 approached, we still had some houses on hand, and we put on a campaign to clean up our inventory. We thought up a good stunt. We decorated one of our houses as a Christmas present—put huge red ribbons around it, with a big bow in front and a Santa Claus on top. Oh, we had it gift-wrapped. And we put lights on it and advertised it in the paper. What could be a more wonderful Christmas present for the family than a home of their own?

We sold all the houses we had left, thirty of them, that Christmas. Our first year as a builder ended with a bang. We made about $20,000.

We didn't let up after our successful first year in business. We were on fire, burning up with ambition. Our motto for 1941 became "A house a day."

I got another basic floor plan to add to our first one, and that gave us even greater variety in developing subdivisions. The great majority of the homes we planned were to be priced at $2,999, with FHA twenty- and twenty-five-year loans.

Although the year turned out well for us in the end, we did have a period of trouble—a crisis. We had thirty-two unsold houses on hand, and sales were almost at a standstill. We were in fair shape economically, but we didn't have much cash. Bankers had said to us that unless we sold some of those houses within two weeks they could not go along with us any further. The FHA said the same thing.

I went home greatly disturbed and talked the situation over with Alma, and we prayed about it. Then she came up with a suggestion, as she usually did in emergencies.

"Call a meeting of all the people who work for us and with us," she said. "Let's get them all together for a little party—carpenters, painters, paperhangers, plumbers, brickmasons, laborers, all of them with their wives, white and colored. Let's give them the facts and tell them that unless we sell some of those houses within two weeks we will have to close up and they will be out of jobs."

I called the meeting, gave each one a Coke, and got

down to business. I explained the situation and passed out lists of the unsold houses.

"I want every one of you to talk about these houses wherever you go," I said. "Tell people what a bargain they are, how nice they are. Talk about them at the drugstore, the grocery, at church, up and down the streets wherever you meet people. Say to your grocer, 'Mr. Grocer, I work for Wallace Johnson. Unless he sells some houses he has on hand, he can't build any more, and I'll be out of a job and can't pay you the money I owe you. If you know of anybody who might buy a house, please tell us.' " And I suggested that they tell their landlords and others the same thing. It worked. It was almost a miracle! Our carpenters, painters, laborers and other workmen sold those houses for us, and we got up full steam again.

Speaking of meetings with all our workmen and our office staff: We found that it helped to have get-togethers frequently. Such parties promoted teamwork and friendship, pride in our projects, loyalty.

At these meetings I made talks in which I tried to give our people good advice about saving a part of their wages and becoming homeowners themselves, and I tried to create within them an interest in all the fine things of life, spiritual as well as material. At one meeting, for instance, I went through all of our canceled payroll checks for the past few weeks. I had them with me.

"We have a fine organization and you are good workmen," I said, "but I find that a good percentage of these checks have been cashed at liquor stores. That leads me to believe that many of you are spending money for whiskey that might better be spent on your families." Then I did a little preaching.

I am happy to report that my little sermon changed the lives and habits of some of them, as did talks I made at other meetings. I was not ashamed to talk to them about improving their lives, talk about morality and religion. I recognized their right to live their own lives, and I never made religion or church affiliation a condition of employment. But as a Christian and as their employer, I felt I had a right and a duty to speak to them as I did. Most rightly construed my talks as a genuine interest in their welfare, not as meddling in their private affairs.

I showed my interest in them in other ways, too. I made it my business to know every employee by name and to know when his birthday was. I sent him a card with a dollar bill attached to it. I also knew his wife and their children. If some of them got sick, we helped look after them. We took pictures of them in little family groups and at our parties. We really tried to be their friends, not just their employers.

We were going along wonderfully well in 1941—till the FHA sent a smart lawyer down here. He came to me and said: "Mr. Johnson, you have been violating the FHA law each time you have sold a home for $2,999, and for each violation you are subject to a fine of ten thousand dollars and ten years in jail." He scared me nearly to death. What had I done wrong?

Well, I had been getting 90 percent loans, $2,700 on $3,000 houses. But I was selling the houses for $2,999. The made the $2,700 loan a little more than 90 percent and illegal.

So I raised my price to $2,999.99 and kept going. That made the $2,700 loan so close to 90 percent of the sale price that anybody who quibbled over it would have seemed silly.

In view of prices today, you may think that our $2,999.99 houses were shacks without modern conveniences, but they weren't. You could do a lot with a dollar back there just before World War II began. But, of course, they were modest homes for low-income people.

I have told you how, as a boy carpenter, I felt called to build houses—called by God to my task just as ministers are called to theirs. And as Alma and I started our own business, I felt that our mission was to build for poor folks and help them own their homes. In that way we could help them to live better, happier lives, for homeownership does lift a man to a higher plane. There is no question about it.

That was the spiritual side of our thinking. On the practical side, I saw more opportunity in the small-home field. The idea of making a small profit on houses and selling lots of them appealed to me more than that of making a big profit on a few. We loved the excitement, the furious activity, the challenge of the volume projects. I enjoyed dashing across town, from one subdivision to another. I was still the little kid with an envelope sticking out of his britches pocket, pencil behind his ear.

It took hundreds of workmen to carry on such a tremendous building program, as you can imagine. Alma and I were on the go from daylight to midnight. We'd drive around, inspecting jobs, or showing homes to prospective buyers, till ten, eleven and sometimes till twelve o'clock at night.

We lived up to our motto in 1941. We built a house a day. It was another good year.

9

YOU'RE IN THE
SEABEES NOW

War brought great changes in home-construction problems and opportunities. A lot of things were reversed. It was no trouble at all to find purchasers of homes, especially in cities and towns where there were military posts and airfields. Homes were in great demand. There were waiting lists of customers. We didn't need salesmanship in selling. We needed it in buying. I mean in finding and buying building materials and in getting government permits to build.

Our business entered a period of furious expansion. We opened offices and started home-building projects in Pine Bluff, Arkansas, and in Batesville, Grenada and Greenwood, Mississippi, while still growing in Memphis. As I look back on it now, I just don't see how we stood up under the killing pace, either mentally or physically. Well, we couldn't have without the help of the Lord. As was my custom, I made lists of our needs and problems and prayed over them. When desperate for lumber, I asked the Lord to guide me to it. When I needed men, I asked Him to help me find them. When I needed loans, I asked Him to send me to the right bankers. And He did.

I'd spend Mondays checking our projects in Memphis, getting them under way for the week. Tuesdays—sometimes on Wednesdays—I'd get into my car and rush away on our circuit—Batesville, Grenada, Greenwood, Pine Bluff—where we had hundreds of homes under construction. I drove a black Ford and almost made it fly. I'd check every house and see what materials were needed, arrange to get the stuff, sign the payroll checks, make out drafts for money, smooth personnel problems, help recruit labor. That would have to be done in each of those four towns, and still I'd have to get back to Memphis in time to meet the payroll on Saturday. I was lucky when I got four hours of sleep a night. Twenty-hour work days were common.

And all the while Alma was working just about as hard in the office in Memphis and out on the projects.

Let me give you an example of how God answered my prayers when I asked Him to help me find lumber. I firmly believe that what happened was an answer, although cynics may attribute it to mere chance.

Alma finally reached the point where she just had to stop and rest, and to get away from it all she went over to Hot Springs, Arkansas, for a few days. Well, that week, after I finished checking the Pine Bluff construction, I decided to drive to Hot Springs to see her. I was in a hurry, as always, and thought I'd try a short cut over some back-country roads—and got lost.

As I crossed a railroad, wondering where I was, I saw one of the most exciting sights I have ever seen—a sawmill with a lot of lumber stacked in the yard around it and with some beautiful standing timber nearby! For a moment I feared it was a mirage. I was down to a two-week supply of lumber, and maybe I was seeing things, just as a lost, thirsty traveler in the desert sees a lake.

Two boys gave me the thumb for a ride just as I crossed the railroad, and I stopped. I asked about the sawmill. They said it belonged to a man who had died, and the widow and daughter were putting it up for sale. I picked up the boys and raced on to Hot Springs.

The next morning I was back at that mill, and I quickly closed a deal for the whole property—mill, about one million feet of lumber, mules, some standing timber. I gave the widow a check for the whole amount. The outlay of so much money at one time put a strain on my finances, for I had payrolls to meet. So I worked like mad, getting all the lumber away from there and on construction jobs. I knew that would make it easier for me to get a loan from a mortgage banker—easier than if the lumber had been standing in an Arkansas lumberyard. So I hauled lumber night and day, and in three or four days I had it well distributed. I got a loan, and my bank account was well fortified.

That wasn't the only sawmill I bought in those frantic early war years. I had learned a lot about sawmills during the time I worked as a shipping clerk at the mill near Pine Bluff—the place where I was fired, you may recall—and I knew what mills cost and how they operated. So when I got a tip that a sawmill at Potts Camp, Mississippi, might be available. I rushed down there and bought it for $160,000 cash. I soon found out why the owner sold it. There wasn't enough timber nearby to keep it busy. But we solved that problem. We dismantled it and moved it to south Mississippi, where there was plenty of timber, and soon had it whining away, turning out the lumber I just had to have.

I became interested in the Home Builders Association

and in 1942 was invited to be on a panel at a meeting in Chicago. Stories about our $2,999.99 house had been printed in real-estate journals and home-builders magazines, and I was asked to come and tell the˙ whole story. Alma helped me prepare my materials—pictures of our subdivisions, drawings of our houses, showing how many different ways you could turn a floor plan around without changing the basic construction, how we standardized to use the most economical lengths of lumber and prevent waste, and so forth. I also had little models of our homes.

Well, the meeting was in the ballroom of the Hilton Hotel in Chicago, and I was telling our story. Sitting near Mrs. Johnson in the audience were three or four men from one company, and one of them was making scoffing remarks.

"I don't believe a word that man is saying," he said. "I'll bet the purchasers of his houses have to use a little outhouse for a bathroom."

Alma stood his cynicism as long as she could, and then she let him have it. She reached over, touched him on the sleeve and said, "Let me say something to you, please. That man you are speaking of happens to be my husband, and he is not lying. He is telling the truth. And for your information, let me tell you that the roofing and other products of your company have gone into every one of our houses. But I have news for you. No more of your products will go into our houses."

You can imagine how shocked and embarrassed that man was. Such profuse apologies came from him and his company that we finally relented and did business with them again. And they couldn't be nice enough to us after that. I never called on them for anything that they wouldn't do readily. We certainly made lemonade out of the lemon that man tossed our way.

At that Chicago meeting I met Henry Kaiser, the famous industrialist, who was one of the principal speakers. I'll never forget something he said during his speech.

"All you reporters get out your pencils," he said. "I'm going to give you the secret of my success." I was sitting near the reporters, and believe me, they quit eating their dessert and pulled out their pencils. "The secret of my success is my home," Mr Kaiser said. "In our home God does abide. And in that home I have the dearest, sweetest wife that a man ever had and a perfect family."

He impressed me as a man with the proper attitude toward life, a man with a proper sense of values.

I had the pleasure of being with Mr. Kaiser many times after our meeting in Chicago, and Kemmons Wilson, my partner, and I became associated with him in a large project in Orange County, California. We enjoyed his friendship and were inspired by his philosophy through the years and right on up to the time of his death. We had the privilege of being in his home and seeing what a wonderful relationship he had with his family.

Anyway, I came away from the Home Builders meeting in Chicago with new enthusiasm about home construction and with the ambition to become more active in the national association—an ambition I was to realize and which was to mean much to me in later years.

All during the war years the problem of getting priorities on building materials and permits to build houses continued. Unless you could find materials not controlled by the government, you were restricted in your programs. Some builders went into the black market for materials, but that was illegal and dishonest. I could not consider doing that, so I prayed and hunted for solutions to the problems.

One day, while going out of my way to do a little hunting, looking at property and anything else that might be bought and used to advantage, I found an old, abandoned sawmill in North Memphis. I made inquiry and bought it for three thousand dollars.

The next day I put a crew on it to clean up the place. It was an unsightly mess. And I sold the junk for three thousand dollars! Stuff that I would have hauled away to the dump.

In the lumber I had bought I found some long timbers —100-foot twelve-by-twelves and sixteen-by-sixteens. I was the only man in the country who had timbers like that, and I got from seven hundred dollars to one thousand dollars apiece for them.

I used some of the other lumber I got with the old mill to build a large shed at our Rayner Street plant.

So out of my frantic search for lumber came one of the best windfalls I have ever had.

Along about that time a friend, Rip Greer, real-estate man, called me up.

"Wallace," he said, "where the Army depot is being built there are fifteen or twenty houses that must be sold and moved within thirty-six hours. Suppose we take a look and see what we can do."

We inspected them—and bought them for one hundred dollars each. Then I went to Orgill Brothers and bought two dozen Skilsaws, the largest I could get. I got my trucks over on the grounds and told my men to start sawing on those houses every twelve feet. I didn't care what they hit, just keep sawing. Saw, saw, saw.

As they would saw off twelve feet of a house, I would have the section loaded on a truck. When we had a load, the driver would take off for some lots we had in North Memphis. We'd keep all the parts of one house together, and our carpenters at the lots would reassemble them. It wasn't too difficult. Soon we had houses on all our lots. Then we had a problem. We didn't have any more lots. Where could we put the other houses?

I remembered the days when I put up signs on lots I didn't own. So we just started reassembling those houses on vacant lots wherever we could find them in the area. We didn't have time to look up the owners and get permission or make a deal. We had to get those houses moved in thirty-six hours, and we knew that if we didn't reassemble each house immediately after we cut it up, the parts would get scattered, and it would be an expensive operation to get the puzzle worked out.

You can imagine the shock of some of those property owners when they saw houses had been erected on their lots. But we were able to make satisfactory deals with them. One fellow came to me and said sarcastically, "Thank you for putting a house on my lot." He meant to keep it without paying for it and to forbid us to come on his property to get it. He was in a good legal position, too. All I could do was just look at him. But he finally softened, and let us have the lot at a fair price.

We sold every one of those houses in a hurry, for, as I have pointed out, selling was no problem in those war days. Rip and I made between eight thousand dollars and ten thousand dollars apiece on the whole deal in a very few days.

The war economy brought an end to our $2,999 houses. We started building larger and more expensive homes.

The Navy selected Millington, Tennessee, a few miles north of Memphis, as the site for the construction of a Naval Technical Training Center. It was a rush job—a crash program. All contractors in the area were asked to participate. The Navy appealed to our patriotism in getting the job done. We promised to participate, as did others. But only two of us showed up on the day to start. Maybe the others figured they could make more on other projects, or something. But we had given our word, and we meant to keep it.

Among the jobs we did at Millington was the construction of homes and apartment houses with a total of 790 units for Navy men. The Navy operations have been continued and expanded since then. Millington is now a city of about fifteen thousand, and we are proud that we had an important part in its development. Our investment turned out well.

Speaking of wartime problems, let me tell you about the crisis that developed at our big wartime building project near Pine Bluff, Arkansas. We bought acreage and developed a subdivision. The government would let us sell only about a third of the homes, or less, on the open market. We had to hold the others to rent to war workers. The problem of finding and keeping workmen was a terrific one. The Army finally drafted every painter we had except one. I was depressed as I went to the office and told Alma the distressing news.

"I just don't see how we are going to make it," I said. "I fear this may be the straw that breaks the camel's back."

But Alma, bless her heart, always keeps calm in an emergency and can usually come up with a good idea. She said just give her a little time and she would think of something. And in less than an hour she had the answer.

"I have noticed in the paper that women are being called on to do all kinds of war work," she said. "I don't know why a woman can't be a painter. I know I've done enough painting around the house."

That night I called C. M. Jolly, our superintendent at Pine Bluff. "Alma has come up with an idea," I said. "Put an ad in the paper there. It should say: 'Wanted, women to paint houses. We pay you while you learn.' "

I said we would pay them forty cents an hour the first week (which wasn't bad pay then), fifty cents the second week, and on up to eighty cents. I told him to buy every applicant a pair of overalls and a paintbrush and let them paint on two or three of our houses, under the direction of the one painter we had left. He was to be the instructor. Let the women paint, give them a rest period and some instruction, and then let them paint some more.

Alma and I drove over to Pine Bluff several days later to see how it was working out. Jolly had forty women in our painting school, and they were a sight to behold. They had paint all over themselves and in their hair, but they were in earnest about it. They weren't just playing. And they developed into some of the best painters we had ever had. They did a beautiful job for us there in Pine Bluff, and it gave us the idea of recruiting women for our projects in Mississippi and in Memphis. It wasn't long before we had not only women painters all over the lot but also women carpenters and even plumbers.

In building 150 homes in that first subdivision at Pine Bluff, we had other problems. One of them was that of obtaining pipe for our water systems. Metal materials were awfully hard to get during the war. I borrowed some two-inch pipe and put it down, but, of course, that was entirely too small for such a large number of houses. It wasn't uncommon for people to stick their heads out their windows and yell to the neighbors, "Hey, cut your water off so I can get a drink!"

Finally, I found some old pipe in a field near Little Rock, and we dug it up and used it to give more volume. You had to use what you could find in those days of scarcity.

I, of course, had to have help in finding enough materials to hold our labor force and keep our projects moving. I had my hands full trying to find enough money to meet payrolls of $150,000 a week or more and couldn't spend too much time hunting and purchasing materials. So we put A. E. Neal in charge of our purchasing department, and he did a splendid job. And by that time Alma's brother, Barney McCool, had joined us full time, and he was a big help. Barney is the one, you may recall, who said I had worked him nearly to death when I was manager of the lumberyard at Itta Bena, Mississippi, and he was a schoolboy on a summer job under me.

Although we had a splendid organization in those war years, we did have some personnel problems. Let me give you an example or two.

Working for us at Grenada, Mississippi, was a very bright young man who had expressed some interest in joining the Seabees, and he finally let the desire get completely out of hand. He went to New Orleans for a weekend of pleasure, and while there he drank something that put big ideas into his head. He went to see the Seabees and happened to talk to the man in charge of signing up whole construction organizations. So right then and there he elected himself a vice-president of Wallace E. Johnson Enterprises and volunteered the whole Johnson organization for service in the South Pacific! Yes, sir! He would take us all to the Pacific as one big group and win the war.

I didn't know about it at the time, but about a week later I received a call from an officer in the Seabees. He said he had completed an inspection of all our equipment at Grenada—trucks, tractors, bulldozers—and had a list of the employees, and he'd come on to Memphis to confer with me and complete arrangements to ship us out of New Orleans right away.

I didn't know what in the world the man was talking about. That was crazy talk. "Wait a minute!" I said. "Who are you and what is this all about?"

He said our vice-president had signed up the Johnson organization in the Seabees, and he was coming on to Memphis. I said, well, come on, for we certainly had things to talk about.

That was about ten o'clock in the morning. I called my wife into the office and told her about the strange call, and we sat there looking at each other and wondering what it could mean. We didn't know whether we were subject to some new war measure or not.

Grenada is only a hundred miles from Memphis, and it didn't take the Seabees' commanding officer long to get here. He said our vice-president had signed up the Johnson organization—the whole caboodle, including our divisions in Arkansas and Tennessee as well as in Mississippi—and the matter had been referred to Washington and approved. Special ships had been ordered to pick us up in New Orleans.

"There's just nothing else for you to do now but go through with it," he said.

I said, well, there certainly was something else for me to do. The young man who had signed us up wasn't an officer in our organization and didn't own a dime's worth of it. He was just a shipping clerk at Grenada. Furthermore, I had large construction projects going that were important to the war effort, and we couldn't think of abandoning them. But, you know, the fellow was stubborn. He still didn't want to take "No" for an answer, because he had gotten himself into a spot. I had to get my lawyer and our senators to help get the crazy business straightened out.

I fired the self-appointed vice-president—again. I think it was about the fourth time I had fired him. But he was

such a good shipping clerk—one of the best I ever saw—
that in a few weeks I hired him back.

Some time later he did join the Seabees. That time he
didn't try to take all of us in with him, though.

Well, that was one kind of personnel problem. We had
other kinds, of course.

One day I had a call from one of my men in Pine Bluff.
He thought he ought to tell me about a young man I had
been especially interested in because he had shown outstanding ability. He had come to us from another construction organization where he had been a truck driver
and then a shipping clerk.

"He's about to get in trouble over here," my co-worker
said. "It involves a girl and is causing talk."

"Oh, my gosh!" I said. "That boy is married and has two
or three children here in Memphis. I'm driving to Pine
Bluff tonight. Tell that young man I want to see him at
the hotel."

He met me there, and I got a room on the sixth floor
and told him to come on up, I had something I wanted to
talk to him about. As he walked into the room, I locked the
door—making sure that he saw me—and then walked to
the window and threw the key out.

He looked at me in astonishment. "What did you do that
for?" he asked.

"Well," I said, "I don't know how many hours we'll be
here, but I'm going to do my best to change your attitude
before we walk out of here."

We had prayer, and we talked. I told him about the
reports I had received. Finally, about two o'clock in the
morning, he broke down and said, "Mr. Johnson, what you
have heard is true, but you don't have all the facts. Still,
you have as much as I want you to know."

He vowed to strike a new course and he did. First,

though, I had to call the room clerk to come up and unlock my door so the young man could get out.

In a few months he was called into military service. Before he left, I told him of the importance Jesus Christ played in my life and I tried to interest him. However, he went into service without making a Christian commitment.

After he came back from service he did accept Christ and joined one of our fine churches. Before he passed away he became one of America's outstanding Christian laymen. He left his family a nice home and great wealth—spiritually and materially.

10

TOP-SECRET

ASSIGNMENT

The telephone call from the Seabees officer excited me, but another call excited me even more during those furious war years.

One day the *Memphis Press-Scimitar*—or maybe it was the *Commercial Appeal*—had a headline which said: "Wallace Johnson Turning Out a House Every Two and One-Half Hours!" And it so happened that General George C. Marshall flew through Memphis that day and saw the paper. A day or two later I got a call from him in Washington. When he told me who he was, I started trembling. I recalled that Seabees business and wondered if I was in for more trouble. If so, I knew I would be in deeper, for General Marshall had a lot of power, and when he gave orders they were obeyed.

He spoke very calmly. "Mr. Johnson," he said, "will you please get your secretary on the line? I want her to make some notes of what I am going to tell you." I got not only my secretary but my wife on the line with me.

"Now, Mr. Johnson," General Marshall said, talking in a slow, pleasant voice, "this is what I would like for you to do. I would like for you and your staff to go to Knoxville, Tennessee, and wait at the Andrew Johnson Hotel for another call." And he named the day we were to leave.

Train reservations were mighty hard to get in those days, and I stammered a bit and said, why, I didn't know that I could get accommodations for all of us.

"Oh, I don't think you will have any trouble with that," he said. "Everything will be arranged for you."

It still didn't register with me that he had all that authority, but a few days later we went to the station as instructed, wondering what in the world it was all about. We found he had taken care of us, all right. There were people begging for a place to ride on the train, any kind of place, and we had a whole car reserved for us.

The next morning we arrived in Knoxville and went to the hotel. Government representatives put us through a pretty rigid examination—asked a lot of questions about our background and then fingerprinted us. Cars came and picked us up and took us out into the country somewhere. We didn't know where we were or what it was all about. We were shown an area where a subdivision was to be built. They wanted three thousand homes constructed in ninety days and no questions asked! Just take the subdivision maps they had prepared and go to work.

Well, that nearly knocked the breath out of me. It was frightening. I started backing away. I explained that I had several thousand houses under construction in Memphis, Arkansas and Mississippi and was hard pressed to get men and materials to finish them. But those government men looked grim and said I had been selected to do that job, and they felt I could do it.

As we left to go home, I was ordered not to tell anybody

about our trip and what was going on. It was top secret.

We went to work on plans for houses to be erected at what we learned later was Oak Ridge, Tennessee, where our great atomic-energy plants were built.

I have forgotten how many homes we designed for the thousands of workers who were rushed there to live in secrecy—a tremendous number—but we had to beg off from the actual construction. I convinced them that we could render a better service to the country by completing the big projects we already had under way. I also pointed out that I owed the banks in the Memphis area so much money that they would have been shocked out of their senses if I had told them I was leaving town.

In those days, when I was rushing around from one project to another, nervous and tense, getting only a few hours' sleep, I was almost a chain cigarette smoker. I often smoked two and three packs a day.

One day Alma and I worked in Memphis till about five o'clock and then got into the car and started for Pine Bluff. We'd do that often—arrive there at night, get up and out on the project early the next morning.

Just before we got into Pine Bluff we came to a big traffic jam. Two fellows had met on a narrow bridge, and neither would back up. There they sat glaring at each other, and traffic stacked up for several miles on both sides of the bridge. Someone went to get the sheriff, but we couldn't do anything but wait and fume. I think we must have sat there two hours!

I was in a stew and smoked nervously. I got careless and almost set the car on fire. We had a little excitement, and I was so embarrassed and exasperated that I said I was through with smoking—positively and forever. It was a silly, expensive habit, and it was dangerous. Besides, I recalled that just a few days before I had read that a man could save ten thousand dollars in a lifetime by not smoking. (It must be more now.)

So I really quit smoking, right then and there, sitting in that traffic jam, wasting time that I could ill afford to lose. After I weathered that storm without smoking any more, I felt victorious.

When we finally got into the hotel in Pine Bluff that night, my brain was really clicking as I thought of the many things we had to remember to do. I had a rule that Mrs. Johnson, her brother Barney or I had to inspect every house we had under construction at least once every week. And when you have hundreds going at one time—well, brother, you have to move.

I made notes furiously in the hotel room that night, and after we went to bed I'd think of other things, get up, turn on the light and write more notes. That disturbed Alma, and she got irked.

"Sweetheart," she said, "if you don't quit turning that light on over there, I-I just don't know what I'll do. I'm so tired. We didn't leave Memphis till five o'clock, and we were tied up at the bridge for hours. Now it's midnight. We've got another hard day ahead of us tomorrow. So go to sleep, for goodness' sakes!"

I decided I had better not turn on that light any more. But my mind kept buzzing with things to remember to do.

In a little while Alma said, "Wallace, do you hear a rat?"

"No, sweetheart," I said, "I don't hear a rat. Go on back to sleep."

In a few minutes she sat up in bed. "Wallace," she said, "are you writing over there in the dark?"

And that's exactly what I was doing, writing like mad in almost complete darkness.

If I can't write in the light, I'll write in the dark. I always have felt the need to write down my goals, to put them on my prayer list. I still do that, and I ask all our key men to do it, too. I can't require them to have prayer lists, but I do have the right to ask them to send me lists of the goals toward which they will strive for the next two weeks. Every two weeks I want new goals. On the back of my own list I always write one of my favorite passages of Scripture: "Ask and it shall be given, seek and ye shall find, knock and it shall be opened unto you."

But let's go back to my resolution to quit smoking. I stuck to it the rest of that trip, and when we got back to Memphis I bought six packs of cigarettes. I scattered them around—on my desk, in my car, in our living room, bedroom, dining room, and I carried one pack in my pocket. When I was tempted to smoke, I said to myself, "Wallace, are you a man or a mouse?" And I remained a man.

I have not smoked a cigarette since that day I decided to quit while sitting in that traffic jam.

I have told you how I took a personal interest in our employees, in their families and problems. Well, in keeping with that, to promote teamwork and friendship, to help us all become better acquainted, and to bring us together for regular meetings at which we could discuss our projects and plans, we organized a club of Johnson employees. I offered a prize of twenty-five dollars to the employee who suggested the best name for the club. The winning name was BOMAH. The initials stand for "Builders of Men and Homes." I liked it because it expressed exactly what I felt my mission in life was.

There came a time, however, when I wondered if my wife and I were smart in sticking to building instead of switching over to farming. During the war we bought the old National Fireworks property in northeast Memphis— fifty-three acres for $22,000. We bought it to hold for future use as a subdivision, since we couldn't start developing it right then and wanted to figure out some use for it that would at least pay the taxes on it in the meantime. So Alma asked me if she could take it over and work out something. I said, why, sure.

Well, she decided to farm it, and I didn't think too much of the idea. I had seen Dad work too hard on the farm and make nothing for his toil. But Alma wouldn't be discouraged. She made a deal with a Negro preacher who lived on the property. He had been a farmer before he felt called to preach. His congregation wasn't paying him too well, and he welcomed an opportunity to supplement his income. Alma was to furnish everything, and he was to do the work, and they'd split the profits.

They decided to plant one third of the acreage in peas, one third in peanuts and one third in sorghum.

The land was fertile, the preacher worked hard, and they had a fine crop. They hired little boys to pick the peas and sold them for $7.50 a bushel, if I remember correctly. I have forgotten what they got for the peanuts, but it was a good price. The big money-making crop, though, was the sorghum. Alma bought an old sorghum molasses mill down in Mississippi and moved it to the property. She and the preacher had their sorghum cane ground and cooked right there on the spot. Sugar, as you know, was rationed, and people were clamoring for substitutes for it. There was a waiting customer for every gallon of sorghum molasses they could produce. People would come to the mill and line up in the afternoon to get the day's production—at $2.85 a gallon.

But Alma wasn't through when they sold their last gallon. The seed heads had been cut off the sorghum stalks as the stalks were prepared for the crushing mill, and she had saved them. Next spring she did a big business selling sorghum seed.

I think she made about eleven thousand dollars in one year on that property. No telling how much she would have made if she had known anything about farming. Made me wonder if maybe we had better forget the development of the tract and let her continue to raise peas, peanuts and sorghum.

Speaking of holding property for future use: Sometimes that can be a little embarrassing.

Edward LeMaster was the real-estate man who sold us the old Fireworks property, and after that he and I sometimes would take rides together. I'd see something I liked, and he'd find out who the owner was and get me a price. He was a fine man to work with like that, a Christian gentleman and a square-shooter.

One day we were riding in North Memphis, just looking, and we came to a tract of ten or twelve acres beside a railroad track that interested me immediately. It was in July and was all grown up in weeds, but it was a pretty sight to me.

"Find out about that property, Ed," I said. "I'd sure like to buy it."

"All right, Wallace," he said. "Do you have any idea what you'd be willing to pay for it?"

"Well, it's between a railroad and a street," I said. "Looks mighty good. I'd say probably two thousand dollars to three thousand dollars an acre. At that price it would be a good buy to hold."

Four days later Ed called me up. "Wallace," he said, "what are you trying to do to me? Are you pulling my leg or something?"

"Ed," I replied, "I don't know what you are talking about."

"It's about that tract in North Memphis you asked me to get a price on," he said. "Why, you've been owning that property five years."

Well, when a man can't resist a likely piece of property, especially one that has potential and is a bargain, and when he buys right and left, it's sometimes a little hard for him to remember everything he has.

I was embarrassed by Ed's report, but I was also pleased. I had unwittingly backed up my first judgment.

Yes, I go for bargains, whether I'm buying real estate or a pair of shoes. I am just a natural-born bargain-hunter. Most of my bargains have been just that, but a few times I have picked up some that weren't. Let me tell you about a real lulu.

I had a large apartment-house development in Greenwood, Mississippi. One day a man came to me and said, "Wallace, I'd like to trade you a six hundred and forty-acre plantation for your apartment house." And I said, "Well, let's talk about it."

I had a debt of $400,000 on my apartment house, and his plantation was clear. But he was willing to swap even. That struck me as a mighty good deal. We closed it.

My head began to swim with big ideas for farming and cattle-raising, and Alma tried to caution me about taking such a deep plunge into a pool with which I was unfamiliar. But I was off and running. I built a fine four-bedroom house, barns and cabins. We also bought some old Army buildings on a nearby discontinued post and moved them to our plantation. In all, I put about $300,000 into buildings, silos and deep wells. I also built a schoolhouse for the Negro children who lived on the place. I got mules and farm machinery, and I planted grass, feed and cover crops and dreamed of going into the cattle business in a big way. Took me about a year to get everything ready. Then I called up a friend, Dr. H. H. Carter, at the South Memphis Stockyards, and I said, "Dr. Carter, I'm ready now to buy a thousand head of steers."

So he went out and started buying steers and shipping them down to my plantation. They weighed between six hundred and eight hundred pounds, and they started running wild and eating their heads off. When they'd come up to be fed, there would be balls of gumbo mud on their tails as large as their heads. But despite all their eating, they lost weight—over two hundred pounds each. The weather was bad, and they ate up all the feed I had been storing away for a year. I became disgusted with the whole venture. I paid 37½ cents a pound for those steers and sold them for 17½.

I lost a fortune on that plantation business. It is my boast that when I find myself with a lemon, I just make lemonade. But I couldn't turn that lemon into refreshment. The only thing I got out of it was acid indigestion.

Occasionally someone asks me why my partner, Kemmons Wilson, and I don't put cattle on some of the tracts of vacant property we own around the country. Huh! I tell them the only beef I'm interested in is the kind you find on the dinner table, not in the pasture.

I attribute my failure in the cattle business to several things. One of them, and probably the most important, was that I was straying from my mission as a BOMAH. I fear I didn't pray about it enough. And I was getting into a business in which I had had no previous experience.

The last year of the war was a furious one for us. We were building harder than ever, and as it began I set new goals toward which to strive. I had seen the need for better housing for Negro citizens, and that was on my mind and heart. It was a great problem. On January 1, 1945, I took it and other problems to the Lord. As always, He heard and answered our prayers. Our problems—whatever they are —have a way of diminishing when we take them to God.

Instead of building two thousand units that year, we built three thousand. Instead of ending the year with $250,000 cash, we ended with $450,000 in the bank. The way for the development of modern but low-priced homes for Negroes did start to open up. And although I didn't reach all my goals that year, I did go on and reach them eventually.

During the year we built many apartment houses and homes priced far above our $2,999.99 house which achieved fame in 1940 and 1941. But as soon as the war ended, we started building for low-income people again. We went back to our $2,999.99 home in simplicity and economy, although the price of materials and labor made it necessary that we sell it for about $7,000.

In driving around Memphis, I kept thinking about the deplorable conditions under which many Negroes lived. They lived in unpainted shacks without bathrooms and other necessities. Many houses were unscreened and were in low areas that flooded in bad weather.

Joe Fowler, director of Memphis Housing Authority, was concerned, too. Many of the tenants in their publicly owned better housing apartments were people whose incomes had risen so much during the war that they no longer were eligible to stay in the subsidized units. But Joe couldn't turn them out. There wasn't any decent private housing for them to go to.

He tried to interest me in developing subdivisions for Negroes. And Buck Horner, director of the FHA for Tennessee, also urged me to do something about the situation.

"Wallace," he said, "you once built a good house for three thousand dollars. See what you can do about building houses and apartments for Negroes to rent for thirty-one-fifty for one-bedroom units and thirty-seven-fifty for two bedrooms."

So, spurred on by Joe and Buck, I started figuring and planning. The lowest I could get it was $33.50 and $41.00.

But that was only the beginning of the solution to the big problem. Even though the FHA would guarantee the mortgages, it wasn't easy to talk the banks and mortgage brokers into lending money on long terms for the construction of Negro houses. Prior to that, Negro shacks had been built for just a few hundred dollars and rented for fifteen dollars or twenty dollars a month. They soon paid for themselves, and it wasn't hard to get financing.

We also had other difficult selling jobs to do. We had to persuade city officials to make utilities available to our Negro subdivisions—lights, water, sewerage, transportation. We had to point out the need for new schools and playgrounds near our homes.

Then, too, we had to reassure white residents near the sites of our proposed developments that we were going to build attractive little homes for people who would take pride in them and that property values would not be depressed.

Oh, it took a lot of salesmanship and diplomacy to get the ground ready for the start of our first subdivision for Negroes. I selected some desirable acreage out on the edge of town. My white advisers thought it was an ideal site, but a Negro businessman and friend didn't agree.

"No," he said, "I don't think this is the place. Too far out. Negroes like to live close to other Negroes, close to their churches and lodges, and close to stores."

I respected his judgment, so I gave up on that site and selected another one nearer the heart of the city, right next to a slum area. We called it Vandalia Homes and started work. It was the first private-capital project for Negroes in

Memphis with mortgages guaranteed by the FHA. Our units consisted of one- and two-bedroom apartments equipped with mechanical refrigerators, gas stoves, hot-air gas heat, modern bathrooms, Venetian blinds. We built 170 units, and we had them all rented before we finished them. Hundreds of Negro families wanted them. We were almost mobbed by them in their eagerness to sign up.

Reaction to the Vandalia project was so favorable that I decided to expand it. Across the street was a five-acre tract on which about fifty families lived in hovels, and that seemed to be the very spot on which to build homes for the Vandalia overflow. The whole tract wasn't owned by one person, and that slowed us down a little. We had to deal with a number of people. Still, we didn't have any trouble agreeing on prices till we called on an old Negro woman known to her neighbors as Miss Ada. Miss Ada's shack was a sorry sight—looked as if a strong wind would make it collapse—but she owned it, and it was home, and she wasn't fixin' to sell it. Naw, sir, she just wasn't interested. She loved that little place.

We offered her more money than we had paid anybody else, and we pleaded for her to cooperate for the betterment of the neighborhood. But Miss Ada was stubborn. I also suspected that she was shrewder than most people gave her credit for being. Her lot was in the middle of our main street. It was a sort of key lot, and we felt we just had to have it to carry out our plans. Maybe Miss Ada saw she had us across a barrel.

Finally, I turned the problem over to Ham Smythe, our trouble-shooter. I told him to go and make a deal with Miss Ada and not to come back till he had a deed to her lot.

He and Miss Ada sparred around for some time and then agreed on a deal. Ham found her another and more desirable lot up the street from our development. He swapped her that for her lot in the tract we wanted. He moved her house to the new location, put it in good condition and gave her two thousand dollars cash.

"Mr. Ham," Miss Ada said when everything had been completed, "I think this is right nice of you all."

Miss Ada was somewhat of a sentimentalist, but I think she also was a pretty smart materialist. She was such a good trader that I would have made her an offer to join our organization if she had been younger.

We immediately started other low-priced projects for Negroes—Carver Homes, Lincoln Apartments, Tunica Homes, Yale Homes. We both sold and rented houses. Many of our tenants were people who had had to move out of public housing because their incomes of more than three thousand dollars a year made them ineligible to remain. And when they moved out to our new homes and apartments, others, who could qualify, moved into the vacated public-housing units. So our building program made it possible for thousands to step up to a better standard of living, one way or another.

Our first subdivision for Negroes attracted national attention. With the cooperation of the newspapers, we called it a low-rental housing project and clinic and invited housing authorities from Washington and builders from all over to come and see what we had done. They came, and it was a great success.

One day while I was trying to sell the whole community on the idea, I attended a civic-club luncheon and sat at a table with a prominent doctor. I told him about our Carver subdivision and suggested that he let me take him out there after the meeting and show him what we were doing. I had a very definite purpose in mind, for a few days earlier, while doing a little investigating in a slum area near us, I had made a discovery.

After the luncheon we got into my car and I drove by the slum area first. I stopped in front of a dilapidated three-room shotgun house. About half the windows were out, there were holes in the little porch, and there was an outside toilet. The only available water was a hydrant three doors down.

"Come on," I said to the doctor. "I want you to look inside this shack."

There wasn't anyone at home, so we pushed open the door and looked in. You could see daylight through cracks in the wall. The ceiling was about to fall in.

"I just want you to see the kinds of homes some of our citizens have to live in," I said. "This is why I'm trying to build better homes for them and why I need all the cooperation I can get."

He was shocked. "Can this be true?" he asked. "Who lives in a shack like this?"

"A Negro woman named Mary Smith," I said. That wasn't her real name, but I'll call her that.

"That's funny," he said. "The woman who works for us is named Mary Smith. Been with us ten years. Almost like a member of the family."

"That's exactly why I brought you here," I said. "The woman who cooks for you and helps to look after your children lives in this place."

"My God, Wallace!" he said. "I had no idea."

Tears began to run down his face, and he reached for his handkerchief.

"Come on," he said, "show me a nice new two-bedroom house I can rent for her."

I did, and a few days later Mary Smith moved into decent quarters.

It took a lot of money to finance our big projects, but I have never been afraid of debt. If you are going to hire money to put to work for you, you've got to get used to being in debt. Not long ago a friend asked me why I got up so early and went to work and why I stayed on the job such long hours. I said, "Man, if you had to pay twenty-five thousand dollars a day in interest on your debts, you'd get up early and hump it all day, too."

I recall a time, though, back in 1948, when I did get a little frightened. I owed a bank $1,750,000, and I couldn't pay it. I walked into the bank, feeling licked, and said to the president: "Here are the keys to my business. Take it over. I can't pay you."

He said: "Put those keys back in your pocket. If you can't run the business, I know I can't."

"Well," I said, "if I'm to continue, I'll have to have four hundred and fifty thousand dollars more to meet my bills."

He let me have it.

11

A DREAM
COME TRUE

I got used to asking for bigger and bigger loans, especially after Kemmons Wilson came into the picture. It was about this time that I got the phone call from Kemmons that led to our arrangement to become partners in the motel business.

After that decision I had a new ball in the air, as if this old juggler needed any more. One of the first things we did to promote Holiday Inns was to get out a letter to seventy-five well-known home builders scattered across the United States. It was a rather mysterious letter, a teaser, for we invited them to come to Memphis, at their own expense, to see something we had to show them. We didn't tell them what it was but said it was important to them and their future.

Sixty-five accepted the invitation. They were in Memphis three days, and we kicked ideas around constantly. Kemmons and I were trying to sell them franchises, but actually we didn't have any to sell. We had moved so fast that we hadn't yet gone through the necessary legal procedures and hadn't had any franchise certificates printed. Our lawyers were flabbergasted by our speed.

We didn't do a very good job of selling at those conferences, but our enthusiasm remained high. Only four of the builders bought franchises. They paid five hundred dollars each for them and signed contracts agreeing to pay the parent company a royalty of five cents a night per room, plus two cents a night for advertising.

To get the company moving, we decided to allocate the franchise fees to the advertising account.

The Holiday Inns headquarters, at first, were in Kemmons' real-estate office on Summer Avenue in Memphis. We had one desk. Later, in 1956, we moved to an old plumbing shed at the Wallace E. Johnson Enterprises offices at 875 Rayner. And soon two stalls in the lumberyard were enclosed to increase the size of the office.

During the first six or seven years of our operation we had a terrific struggle. We were laboring under the misconception that the Home Builders of America were the people to work with, and we weren't getting anywhere with them. We had a model of a Holiday Inn made and took it to the Home Show in Chicago. That attracted the attention of the public and helped, even if it didn't sell the Home Builders.

So Kemmons and I decided to look elsewhere for people to join us in building a motel chain. We saw that we needed a capable executive vice-president to run the office, coordinate all our efforts, carry out our ideas, push the expansion program. And one fine day in 1955, while sitting under a tree drinking soda pop, we suddenly realized we had our man.

It was at the annual picnic of the local Home-Builders Association, and Kemmons and I got to talking with William

B. Walton, attorney for the association. We told him what we were trying to do, about our dream of a national chain of Holiday Inns and about our difficulties. We had put into it all the money we could get, but we hadn't gotten very far. Still, we were convinced that the idea would go over big if we could just get it off the ground and flying. We desperately needed to find the right man to come in with us and tie everything together.

We were just talking, sitting there under a tree at the Italian Club where the picnic was held. Neither Kemmons nor I could get very far away from our dream in our conversation. Bill Walton was a friend and good listener.

Suddenly it occurred to us that the man we were looking for was right there drinking soda pop with us. Bill had a good law practice, a fine home, was doing well. He had a substantial income and was happy in his profession. So, at first blush, the suggestion that he push aside the security he had and join up with an outfit that was practically broke, run by two visionaries—well, that struck him as a little absurd. Why should he take such a gamble?

But as we talked on he caught our enthusiasm and our vision. Sure, we agreed, he would be taking a risk if he came in with us, but every big undertaking involves some risk. If we all worked hard and put the thing over on a national scale, we'd have a lot of fun and make sizable fortunes.

We leveled with Bill. If he became our executive officer, he would have to work full time at the job—long hours. And we couldn't begin to match the income he had. The best we could promise him was enough to live on—enough to buy bacon and eggs. Kemmons and I would continue to scrape around for a little money, and between us we could assure him of five hundred dollars a month.

Bill accepted our offer and our challenge. He was cold sober, too, for, as I say, we were drinking soda pop.

The agreement was that he was to join us officially on January 1, 1956. That would give him several months to close out his law practice and other interests. But we had him so fired up that he didn't wait for his official connection to begin. He started planning at once.

He became our executive vice-president and did a great job all through those hard, trying, formative years. He deserves much of the credit for the success of our organization. And, of course, the gamble he took in 1955 has paid off handsomely for him.

In 1969, when I moved up to vice-chairman of the board so that I would have fewer administrative duties and more time to devote to our development program, Bill succeeded me as president and continued to be a tower of strength in that position for two years. He then moved up to his present position as vice-chairman of the board.

Well, after Bill joined us, we really began to push our campaign to sell Holiday Inn franchises. We sent Jack Ladd, a top real-estate salesman who had joined us, and Barney McCool, my brother-in-law, out on the road to sell franchises to anybody who would buy. I brought in from a farm in Mississippi an old station wagon for Jack and Barney to travel in. It had been used in the hauling of manure. We repainted it green and yellow and cleaned it up, but we never could get all the manure out of the cracks. The odor wasn't too noticeable when Jack and Barney started out in the cool of the morning, but when it got hot in the middle of the day it was pretty strong. Occasionally they'd stop in the shade on the side of the road and get out of the car to get away from it.

The manure atmosphere probably wasn't good for those boys' morale. It may have tended to depress them and destroy their confidence at a time when they so badly needed shots in the ego to boost their spirits. I fear that on hot days they went in to see prospective purchasers wondering if they smelled like barnyard fertilizer.

But Jack and Barney were real salesmen and they believed in the Holiday Inns dream, and they sold a few franchises during those first years, despite the fact that we were unknown in the motel field and despite other handicaps. But at five hundred dollars a franchise, they didn't make enough to pay their expenses and make a decent living for themselves, with some left over for investment in an expansion program for the Inns. Kemmons and I had put into it every nickel we could spare, and we eagerly awaited the return of Jack and Barney from a selling trip, ready to grab franchise checks. But they needed to keep every dollar they had, and the two of them, with the connivance of Bill Walton, executive in charge of the office, resorted to tricks to outwit Kemmons and me. So you know what those fellows would do? They'd tape franchise checks under the bottoms of their desk drawers, to keep us from finding them before they could get to the bank with them.

After Kemmons and I had put between $300,000 and $400,000 each into the project, we felt we were almost at the end of our rope. We just didn't have any more money. But we all kept scrambling and trying. Barney talked his sister, my wife Alma, into lending him and Jack some expense money, and that helped to keep them on the road. And finally, slowly, the tide began to turn.

Hard, persistent work began to pay off for Barney and Jack. We increased our franchise price from five hundred dollars to one thousand dollars and it was easier to find purchasers at that price than it had been at five hundred dollars.

We went public on August 20, 1957. At that time there

were eighteen franchised Inns and seven owned by the parent company. We sold 120,000 shares of stock at $9.75 a share, and the net proceeds of the sale gave us a check for $1,026,000. That was big enough to make our eyes bulge. I have a framed picture of it in my office. It represents a great day in our history.

I shall never forget an experience I had in connection with the sale of that stock. Bill Walton gave me quite a shock, and he still laughs about it.

The sale was underwritten by Equitable Securities, and when their check for $1,026,000 was handed to us at the closing, we passed it to Bill. Kemmons and I were ready to rush away on a trip, so we told Bill to take the money and invest it for the time being. We would be gone a couple of weeks and when we returned we would decide what to do with it. A million dollars was a lot of money and we wanted to get it to work at once without the loss of even a day.

Well, the next time I saw Bill was on the night of the day on which we returned from the trip. I was driving down the street and recognized his car coming from the opposite direction. So I leaned out and waved him down. He parked on his side of the street, and I pulled to the curb on my side. I jumped out and ran over to his car.

"Hello, Bill," I said. "Just got back in town. How's everything? How did you invest that money?"

"I put it into bonds," he said. "Venezuelan bonds."

I was dumfounded—shocked. We couldn't speculate in South American bonds with that money! We had to build Holiday Inns with it. Had Bill lost his mind? I got so mad I felt like socking him. And as Bill tells it, my face became so red it positively glowed in the darkness.

I demanded an explanation of such an ill-advised investment. What right did he have to do such a thing?

"Why, you told me to take the money and invest it," he said with a hurt look on his face. "That's what I did."

And then I really was fit to be tied. I sputtered, and I guess he feared I was about to have a stroke, so he burst out laughing and confessed that he was just pulling my leg. He had put the million into U.S. government bonds.

Another lawyer friend of ours couldn't take our fast-moving operation with such a light touch of humor. When we were starting out with our campaign to sell franchises, we went to him and said, "John, we haven't any money to pay you for your services in getting our franchise business set up legally, but if you'll become secretary and our counsel, we'll give you a 10 percent interest in Holiday Inns." He said he would accept the offer.

Kemmons and I soon started five Holiday Inns, and if they had all been finished on the same day we would have been short a million dollars. That frightened our lawyer, and he called me one day and said, "Wallace, what in the world are you going to do if you get those things finished?" I said, "Well, I don't know, but I'll work it out some way or other. I've still got a line of credit I can use."

That exasperated him. "But that's not good," he said. "You'll have to pay that money back."

I agreed. "But what do I do?" I asked.

Our lawyer thought Kemmons and I were off our rockers, and he'd call up and protest about what we were trying to do. We'd go 'round and 'round. And finally he started calling my wife, pleading with her to put some sense into my head. He felt we were heading for trouble, doing risky things that he as our lawyer could not approve.

One day after a long wrangle with him I said, "John, you are killing me."

"And you are killing me," he replied.

"Well," I said wearily, "I'll tell you what we'll do. Kemmons and I will buy your 10 percent interest in Holiday Inns for fifteen thousand dollars," and he said it was a deal. There was a tone of relief in his voice.

If he had kept his 10 percent, he would today be a millionaire many times over just from his association with Holiday Inns.

John is still a good friend of ours and still does a lot of work for us as a lawyer. When I kidded him one day about selling out for a song when he could have made millions by holding his stock and sticking with us, he laughed and said, "Wallace, if I had stuck with you and Kemmons and kept up the pace we were going, I'd be dead. I just couldn't stand the pressure."

Anyway, getting back to our going public in 1957, the check for $1,026,000 from the sale of stock didn't last very long in our big plans. We soon found that we needed more money, and we made trips to see investors around the country. But it was hard to get first-mortgage money and hard to get equity money. Kemmons went to a meeting of businessmen in Virginia, called by the President, if I remember correctly, and while there he met a good personal friend of ours, Roger Keyes, who is now executive vice-president of General Motors.

"If you and Wallace want some money," Roger told him, "I believe I can get it for you."

That sounded good to Kemmons, and he called me and said he was going on to New York and see what he could do. Roger, who had returned to New York, took Kemmons to meet a group of investors. They had a long and satisfactory conference, and, as a result, we got $2,500,000 from the group on 5 percent convertible debentures.

Later, from the same group, we obtained another $2,000,000.

They did all right by doing business with us. We paid them cash on their investment, plus interest. They have converted the rest and have Holiday Inns' stock worth many times their investment.

As we kept growing and needing more and more money for expansion, we decided to make a second offering of stock to the public. That, too, was a success.

Then we thought up another idea for getting capital. We approached oil companies with the suggestion that we make a deal for the operation of service stations at Holiday Inns. Certainly the Inns on major highways, catering to the traveling public, would be strategic locations for service stations.

One major oil company said they'd be interested in having stations adjacent to Holiday Inns and would pay us a royalty of one-half cent a gallon for all gas pumped—but only after they had thirty service stations and thirty Holiday Inns tied together. But we never did get the required thirty.

Later we held a conference with the Gulf Oil Company, and this is a matter of public record or I wouldn't be disclosing the business details. The conference was with some of the top Gulf men and was held at a Holiday Inn in Houston, Texas. I'll never forget it, because they were such a fine, pleasant bunch of men to work with. We worked till 2 A.M., and 98 percent of the things that we agreed on tentatively that night was finally approved by both companies.

They agreed to make us a loan of $6,000,000 and to buy $15,000,000 worth of 5 percent preferred stock. They also agreed to give us 100 percent endorsement on mortgages up to $25,000,000.

We also entered into an agreement under which Gulf credit cards could be used for charging food and lodging at all Holiday Inns. That arrangement has been copied by other motel chains and oil companies since then, but we were the pioneers in the field. Our connection with Gulf has been most satisfactory and has been mutually beneficial. One year more than $120,000,000 was charged at Holiday Inns by Gulf card-holders. Hundreds of Gulf service stations have been opened adjacent to Holiday Inns over the years.

Yes, the Gulf people have been very nice to us, and our alliance has worked out well for all of us.

So, with solid backing and encouragement from many sources, and with favorable public response to the services and products we offer, Holiday Inns has grown into the world's largest hotel-motel system. There are more than 1,700 Holiday Inns in operation with more than 278,000 rooms. According to an *Institutions* magazine survey, the Holiday Inns system provides more food and lodging than any other group in the world—except the United States Army!

In August 1968 we celebrated the opening of our one thousandth Holiday Inn, which is in San Antonio, Texas, and the number has continued to increase. A new Holiday Inn is opened somewhere every two or three days. There are approximately 85,000 people employed in the Holiday Inn system. At Holiday City, our headquarters, we have 2,500.

The task of processing up to 820,000 messages a day is handled speedily and efficiently by our computerized Holidex reservation system. We use the equivalent of more than 300,000 miles of communication lines, and through them and satellites we are linked with over 2,300 Holidex reservation terminals.

Our computer equipment also serves our company in other ways, such as the processing of data for all our divisions.

Holiday Inns is expanding rapidly into other countries. It will soon be possible for travelers to go around the world in easy jumps, stopping off at Holiday Inns, with reservations for the whole trip confirmed in advance. Inns are now open in popular tourist destinations such as St. George, Bermuda; Honolulu, Hawaii; Freeport, Grand Bahama Island; Rome, Italy; Montego Bay, Jamaica; Acapulco, Mexico; and on the islands of Aruba and Curacao in the Netherlands Antilles.

The Holiday Inn in downtown Toronto, Canada, is the world's largest, with 719 rooms. The second largest is the inn at Waikiki Beach, Hawaii, with 646 rooms.

You will find Holiday Inns in over fifty countries of the world, and we continue to expand each year.

Wallace E. Johnson's parents, Felix Alva Johnson and Ida Josephine Edwards, taken three months after their marriage on November 21, 1900.

Wallace E. Johnson at age five, with his infant brother, Graves.

The 1923 graduating class of Sunflower Agricultural High School, Moorhead, Mississippi; Wallace E. Johnson is in the center of the middle row.

Felix Alva Johnson (1879–1950)

Original headquarters of Wallace E. Johnson, Inc., at 875 Rayner Street, Memphis, Tennessee.

WEJ at his desk at Rayner Street head-quarters.

Christmas party in basement of Rayner Street headquarters, 1954; the late Mr. John Knox, vice-president of Wallace E. Johnson, Inc., as Santa Claus.

Wallace E. Johnson, William B. Walton, and Kemmons Wilson, looking over plans for a Holiday Inn.

Kemmons Wilson and Wallace E. Johnson checking plans for the building of a Holiday Inn.

WEJ with the Great Sign in 1961

September 30, 1963, Holiday Inns is listed on the New York Stock Exchange; from left to right: Keith Funsten (New York Stock Exchange), William B. Walton, Kemmons Wilson, Mrs. Ruby "Doll" Wilson (mother of Mr. Wilson), Mrs. Kemmons Wilson, Mrs. Wallace E. Johnson, and WEJ.

WEJ speaking at the groundbreaking ceremony for an addition to the Sam Houston Memorial Hospital.

Present headquarters of Wallace E. Johnson Enterprises at 3000
Walnut Grove Road, Memphis, Tennessee; construction completed
September 1968.

Night photograph of the Wallace E. Johnson Enterprises Building

Mrs. Walter Magee, president of the General Federation of Women's Clubs, and Wallace E. Johnson, chairman of National Bible Week, present citation of appreciation to Dr. and Mrs. Norman Vincent Peale at the Hotel Pierre, New York.

Wallace E. Johnson as chairman of 1968 National Bible Week.

1968 Religious Heritage of America Awards Program, emceed by WEJ (left); Judge Boyd Leedom (right) presented a Religious Service Citation to Harold Stassen.

Lighting of torch at groundbreaking ceremony for Shoal Creek Hospital in Austin, Texas; from left to right: Mayor Harry Aiken, Mary Gillen, Dr. Theo Painter, Alma E. Johnson, and WEJ.

WEJ receives a 1968 Horatio Alger Award from Dr. Norman
Vincent Peale.

Celebration in honor of Mr. and Mrs. Johnson on their forty-fifth wedding anniversary; at left is Mr. Johnson's mother, then ninety-one years old.

Religious Heritage of America Awards Conference, 1969; from left to right: Robert P. Gerholz, Mrs. George Romney, George Romney, Mrs. Robert P. Gerholz, Wallace E. Johnson, and Mrs. Wallace E. Johnson.

First home built by WEJ
in 1940; Neil P. Delong,
the owner, stands in front.

Mr. and Mrs. Johnson looking over
plans for their new home.

The Wallace E. Johnson's second
home in Houston, Texas, is a
replica of Mount Vernon.

W. Clement Stone presents an award from Invest in America,
Inc., to WEJ for his outstanding contributions to the free-enterprise
system in America.

WEJ presents Religious Heritage of America Man of the Year Award to Kemmons Wilson, chairman of the Board of Holiday Inns; at left is Mrs. Wilson.

Mr. and Mrs. Johnson with Mr. Johnson's mother, age ninety-four, and Billy Graham at the Wallace E. Johnson Prayer Breakfast during the International Association of Holiday Inns Conference, 1972.

12

NOW THE
WORLD'S
LARGEST

Sometimes I am asked how we go about selecting locations for our company-owned Holiday Inns. Well, location is very important to most businesses, but especially to ours. We study maps and statistics on the growth of areas, keep an eye on the travel picture, watch highway and airport construction, check the motel and hotel accommodations already available in cities and towns.

The best way to find a good location in any given area, we have found, is to make an aerial survey of possible sites. When Kemmons and I were starting our expansion program, we bought a single-engine Bonanza airplane on credit. Kemmons had been a wartime pilot, and we'd get into that little Bonanza and away we'd go winging across the country, peering down, looking for likely locations. Bill Walton sometimes went with us.

Occasionally, after Kemmons got the plane up, leveled off and pointed in the right direction, he would turn the controls over to me and maybe snooze a little. That would make Bill nervous, because I wasn't a pilot. He says I was the zigzaggingest flyer the world has ever seen.

I'll admit that on one occasion Bill's fears were justified. Sometimes when Kemmons and I saw a piece of property that seemed perfect for a Holiday Inn, we'd get excited over it. He'd look down at it from his side of the cab and point and shout about it enthusiastically, and I'd do the same thing on my side. And if we didn't watch ourselves, we'd get so excited we'd forget we were flying a plane. In fact, we forgot completely one day and went into a spin. Down and around and around we went, and Kemmons had to use all his skill to get us out of it.

After we got out of the spin, climbed back up to five thousand feet and leveled off again, Bill, still rather white with fright, demanded to know what had happened. I said, "Ask Kemmons. He was flying the plane." Kemmons looked at me in astonishment. "I thought you were flying it!" he said.

We still fly around the country, looking for locations, attending to other business, inspecting and dedicating new inns, making speeches, but we no longer fly together. Our board of directors advises against that, so that in case of a fatal crash, they won't have to replace all of us at one time. We have a conservative board.

When we fly nowadays, we fly in a modern, company-owned jet, with a crew to handle it. I also have my own plane, with a professional pilot and co-pilot at the controls. I can look down, get excited over a good location without endangering my neck.

Our operations are now so far-flung that we need these newer, larger and faster planes.

In our early years it was our policy to build one- and two-story Inns on the main highways, out from the downtown sections of cities. We still like such locations and aim at having several Inns in the peripheral areas of most large cities. But we no longer stick to that policy exclusively. We now also see the need for at least one downtown Inn in big cities and are trying to fill it. In some cities we have two or more Inns in thickly populated areas where we provide inside parking, some of it underground. These Inns are high-rise buildings, such as the thirty-three-story Inn in Chicago and the eighteen-story Inn in New York.

We also are constructing Inns at famous resorts as well as in commercial and industrial cities. I already have mentioned the 614-room Inn at Freeport, Grand Bahama. We have one of seventeen stories, 400 rooms, at Miami Beach.

Some of our newer high-rise Inns are circular in shape, such as the 174-room Inn in Denver, and one of the same size in Austin, Texas. The round design gives the maximum efficiency in space, with elevators in a center core and rooms fanning out from it. The round shape also provides a maximum of good views from the rooms and balconies.

Our policy is flexible. We build the kind of Inn we think is the most attractive and desirable for the location.

Our fast and phenomenal growth has been accompanied by the development or acquisition of a number of subsidiaries, or operating divisions—some tremendous in size, such as Tco Industries, Inc., and some small, but all an important part of our over-all operations.

Through them we are engaged in many kinds of businesses—transportation, manufacturing, food processing, construction, finance, insurance, services—but all of them tied in with the hotel-motel business.

And the man largely responsible for this vast and successful expansion is the chairman of our board, Kemmons

Wilson. Sure, all of us at headquarters have had a hand in it, but he has been the field general with the imagination and foresight to conceive the program and the know-how to lead us to our objectives.

One of our most recent acquisitions is Tco Industries, Inc. It came to us in a deal involving over $200,000,000 and puts us into the transportation business in a big way.

Tco owns Continental Trailways, the second largest intercity bus line in the United States, and Delta Steamship Lines. We operate 2,500 buses and a fleet of eleven ships.

Through Tco we also have Continental Trailways Tours, Holiday Life Insurance Co., C. T. Life and Accident Insurance Co., Four States Realty Company.

All told, Tco has approximately ten thousand employees.

Through Holiday Inns and Tco, we think we offer a service in the accommodation-transportation field that is without equal.

Although Tco and its line-up of companies is our largest subsidiary, we have others of tremendous size, and they are all growing. The primary function of most of them is to supply both the company and franchised Inns with everything they need, from construction to everyday operation, at advantageous prices made possible by volume purchasing and specialized know-how.

But our subsidiaries and divisions don't do business with Holiday Inns exclusively. They sell products and services to the general public. A dollar made that way is worth just as much as a dollar made renting a motel room. We don't even hesitate to sell to competitors.

Let's take a glimpse of some of our subsidiaries, to give you a better understanding of our operations.

Inn Keepers Supply Company is one of our major divisions. It sells room furnishings of all kinds and food-service equipment—everything a motel operator will need in order to open for business.

Our Holiday Press is another major department. We started it to print our own stationery, bookkeeping and other office forms, and to print our own HOLIDAY INN magazine, a bi-monthly beautifully illustrated in color, designed to promote travel. It has a circulation of 1,250,000. We also print millions of copies of the Holiday Inn Directory, which must be kept up to date.

Now Holiday Press is doing a national business in commercial printing and is a leader in the production of institutional printed forms. Our plant is one of the most modern in the world.

Holiday Press also sells office supplies and office furniture.

A big revenue producer is the Holiday Inn Construction Department, which constructs conventional Inns and high-rise Inns. Right now, for instance, this division has under construction four conventional Inns and one high-rise Inn for the parent company, and fourteen conventional Inns and one high-rise Inn for licensees. It's a large and busy organization.

We have a Special Products Department which markets consumer items under the Holiday Inn label, such as candy, gifts, novelties. This division also handles the Coffee Host program—equipment and supplies for the furnishing of free coffee to guests which they make in their rooms.

An important supplier for our Products Division is the Nat Buring Packing Company, another HI subsidiary. It was a well-known and successful firm when it joined our system, and its King Cotton brand of meats and meat products was favorably known throughout the mid-South. The King Cotton label has been continued, but we also market products under the Holiday Inn label. Buring is supplying several hundred of our Inns with a complete line of meats, sausage, bacon and frankfurters. The business showed a 20 percent increase the first year they came into our organization, as compared to the previous year, and the volume is still going up.

Another big subsidiary is the Institutional Mart of America, which is one of the showplaces of Holiday City. It is a large, attractive building, with an inner court and pool, and has 300,000 square feet of floor space. In it manufacturers, distributors and dealers display everything needed to furnish and operate a motel, hotel, dormitory, restaurant, cafeteria, institutions of various kinds. It is a complete shopping center for buyers. They find everything they need at our IMA—and a lot of things they want when they see them—furniture, fixtures, rugs and carpets, lamps, bedding, paintings and prints, drapes, china and tableware, stoves and utensils, air-conditioners and heaters, mirrors, plaques. And everything is so artistically displayed that the atmosphere is that of a world's fair instead of a merchandise mart.

We opened the Mart late in 1967, and one hundred suppliers had displays with us at that time. The number increased to 210 within a year, and they took all the available space. We now have a waiting list, and we will try to accommodate them as soon as we can make the necessary additions to the building. Buyers from all fifty states and twenty-two foreign countries have visited the Mart.

We have other service divisions, but now let's glance at some of our manufacturing subsidiaries.

In Memphis we have Holiday Woodcraft, which manufactures custom counters and display cases; Master Kraft Manufacturing Company, which provides facilities for different types of refrigeration units; Institutional Mart of America Resources Terminal, known as "IMART," which markets a complete line of supplies for the lodging and food industry under the name of "INNKARE"; Menu Maker Food Service Company, where we process red meats and other foods; Modern Plastics, which makes lamps for the Inns and dry cargo shipping containers; Holiday Containers, where we make corrugated shipping containers.

At Grand Rapids, Michigan, we have Johnson Furniture Company, which manufactures contract furniture, stereo and television cabinets, living-room and dining-room suites.

Our Champion Lighting Company is at Hialeah, Florida, where we make quality commercial lighting fixtures.

And in Chicago we have International Foam, a plant which produces padding for bedding and carpets, upholstery, protective packaging.

In St. Louis, Missouri, and Fort Worth, Texas, is the Bianco Manufacturing Company, where we make all types of commercial seating, particularly for restaurants, lounges, hotel and motel lobbies, hospitals, all kinds of institutions.

Well, so much for manufacturing divisions. Now let's go back to service subsidiaries and complete the list.

We have the General Innkeeping Acceptance Corporation. It assists customers of the other divisions in their secondary financing and is a most important link in the chain of our business.

All Holiday Inns are tied together in a computerized reservation system known as the Holidex network. Our guests, without charge, can make reservations at any Holiday Inn and get instant confirmation.

We also are in the aviation business with HI-Air, another subsidiary. HI-Air sells and operates small planes, an FAA-approved repair station, and offers complete aircraft service—storage, leasing, rental, travel facilities.

When HI-Air joined the Holiday Inn family in 1966, it was a relatively small company doing much less than a million dollars worth of business. This year its revenues will reach about four million dollars.

Its physical size has also increased considerably. At its main location at Memphis International Airport, the company has six hangars, a two-story office building and 310,000 square feet of paved ramp area.

HI-Air has also opened facilities at the Olive Branch Airport, which offer the same fixed-based services as the main facility. The new airport, incidentally, is owned by Holiday Inns and is located on our Holiday Industrial Park.

We are on the air from midnight to 5 A.M. on stations all over the country, with popular, dreamy, soothing music. Our programs are emceed by Dolly Holiday, who in private life is Miss Dotty Abbott. Dotty was a well-known radio personality and vocalist before she joined us. She sings, talks, announces the recorded numbers and tells about Holiday Inns. Her programs are taped and sent to the scores of stations where we buy time.

Some people have asked me why in the world we'd want to be on the air between midnight and daylight. They have the idea that nearly everybody is asleep during those hours and that even the few who are still awake don't listen to the radio. Well, we know how wrong they are. Thousands of people are awake in those early-morning hours, working at all kinds of jobs, driving on the highways, going hunting and fishing, or just sitting up at home because they can't sleep. And we know they like to listen to Dotty because her fan mail is tremendous.

In our program of diversification, we are constantly negotiating for the purchase of new subsidiaries, or we are organizing new divisions from scratch.

It's interesting to be in a business where one thing naturally leads to another. It's fun to try new ideas and make them work.

13

HOW TO GET
MORE DONE

With all of these activities going on, many of my friends used to shake their heads in disbelief. "How in the world can you keep things straight? How can you get everything done?" Well, obviously, I couldn't begin to know the details of every aspect of our businesses; as we grew our need for personnel grew also, and we were blessed with some of the finest business minds of any organization I know. I'll go a step further: They were the finest people, high caliber, dedicated, enthusiastic, talented.

Still, I did try to keep tabs on things, and to do this I had to learn new ways to conserve time and energy. That was the trick, using one's time to best advantage. Most people waste many hours every day on tasks that could be streamlined, delegated, or just eliminated.

Some people would say they felt sorry for me. "Poor old Wallace. Doesn't have any time for fun." My answer was

that I was having fun. I was doing exactly what I enjoyed:
working. My work was my play, and I played sixteen to
eighteen hours a day.

Then these people looked at my responsibilities and
gasped:

* Vice-chairman of the board, Holiday Inns
* Chairman of the board, Medicenters of America
* Chairman of the board, Wallace E. Johnson Enterprises
* Chairman of the board, Alodex Corporation
* Vice-president, Walkem Development Company
* Officer in seventy other corporations

One guy told me I should be slowing down. I told him
he was probably right. I should have been, but if anything
I seemed to be getting more efficient, and all I did was to
keep adding more things to my schedule. It is true that I
moved up from president of Holiday Inns to become vice-
chairman of the board, unloading some of my administrative duties on William B. Walton, who succeeded me, but
I continued to work just as many hours as ever.

But I had no time for golf, hunting, fishing, cocktail
parties, poker games, shows. What a pity!

I did have a couple of small hobbies that I enjoyed for a
few minutes occasionally. I have a miniature train at my
home, and I got a kick out of "railroading." And I collect
small mechanical animals—the kind that you wind up, and
they run and jump around. Such toys fascinate me. When
I was on trips and had the time, I liked to browse around
in toy shops, looking for new animals to add to my menag-
erie. And I tried my hand at such things as golf, but not
very enthusiastically.

Years ago I had a friend, Bill Hill, who was an enthusiastic golfer, and he kept after me to take up the game. It
would do me so much good to spend an occasional afternoon out on the golf course, in the fresh air and sunshine,
away from the cares of business. I was busy and was having

all the fun I could stand, but Bill was insistent. He seemed to regard it as a great humanitarian duty to get me to play golf.

Well, he finally wore me down. So I went to a sporting-goods store and told the owner I wanted to take up golf. What did I need? He said I'd have to have clubs, of course, and I nodded. I knew that much about the game, all right. He sold me about three hundred dollars worth of clubs. Then he said I'd need a bag to carry them in, and that was seventy-five dollars. I asked him what else I needed. He said I couldn't play without balls, and I said give me a dozen. Next he asked about shoes. Certainly I'd need golf shoes. I said O.K., give me a pair of size 13, triple A.

I got all my outfit together and drove out to Chickasaw Country Club. I was already a member but had never played golf and didn't have a locker. I rented one for five dollars a month and put my stuff into it. Then I was asked if I wanted to have my clubs cleaned regularly, as most players did. That would be five dollars a month. I wanted to do the thing right, so I said I'd take the cleaning service.

I left, and that was that. I became even busier in the days and weeks that followed and I never got around to playing golf. I always had something else to do that I thought was not only more important but more fun. My golf outfit remained in the locker forgotten, and my book-keeper continued to pay the rental on it, month after month, and the months stretched into years.

It was five years before those clubs were taken out of that locker! And even then I didn't use them. A visiting Baptist preacher wanted to play golf, and he hadn't brought his clubs with him. His remark reminded me that I had some, and I was delighted to lend him mine. I was sorry I couldn't play with him, but I was happy to make arrangements for him.

When he finished his round that afternoon, the clubs

went back into my locker, and there they remained un-used for another five years! When they were finally used for the second time, it was another visiting preacher who used them, in a situation similar to the conditions under which they had been used the first time.

Once more they went back into the locker, and I con-tinued to pay rent on it for almost another ten years—making about 20 years in all. I finally got self-conscious about the absurdity and gave the clubs to Ralph McCool, my wife's cousin, a golf player. I never hit a ball with any of those fine clubs.

Golf, I know, is a wonderful game. I can understand how many people would love it. But I never felt the need for it and don't feel that I have missed anything by not playing it.

The same goes for hunting.

I'm not a hunter. I don't like to shoot anything. But I have friends who like nothing better than to get out in the woods and fields and bang away.

Once when we were at our home in Hot Springs, Ar-kansas, I heard about a nearby private game preserve. They had lots of quail, and they had hundreds of wild ducks. Hunters paid according to the game they killed—five dol-lars a duck, and so much per quail.

Well, acting on an impulse, I invited a group of business associates and friends, who were enthusiastic hunters, to come over as my guests and shoot on this private preserve. They came loaded with guns and ammunition, and I took them out to the preserve. "Enjoy yourself, gentlemen," I said. "It's all on me."

They hunted quail first and had great luck. They were all crack shots, and I saw my bill mount to ruinous figures.

Then they went for the ducks. Each shooter was placed

on a stand. Ducks were released, trained to fly to the lake. As they went over, the hunters cracked down on them. And they didn't miss—bang-bang! And another dead duck would fall. That went on for an hour or so, and I got much wilder than the poor ducks. Every one that fell was costing me five dollars! And they were having so much sport that they didn't show an inclination to let up! It sounded like a battle.

Finally, I started going from one hunter to another, stealing their shells when they were looking the other way. It was a desperate measure, but it was the only way I could stop them.

Those Dead-Eye Dicks cost me between one thousand dollars and two thousand dollars for quail and ducks. If I hadn't stolen their ammunition, they would have shot me into bankruptcy.

The experience taught me a lesson. Never invite crack shots to be your guests at a place like that. Invite your friends who can't hit the side of a barn.

It's been the same all my life: My work is my play. Even as a small boy I liked to work—or to play like it. I preferred it to playing cops and robbers, cowboys and Indians, preferred it to swimming and hunting. Now that I am seventy-six I still feel the same way.

The thing is, you see, that what is fun for one person may be boredom for another. Work is fun for me. Golf may be fun for you. If I could think of something that would give me a return of more fun and satisfaction on my investment of time, I'd change my schedule and do it.

As a businessman, I must have some understanding of the value of the things in which I invest and trade, and the most important commodity of all is time. Because it is so precious, and because the supply of it is so limited that it is rationed, I try to use every minute to the utmost.

In at least one respect everybody starts the day on an equal basis. We all have the same number of hours—twenty-four. No matter how rich we are, how influential, how smart, we can't buy or borrow an extra hour.

But, my, how people do differ in what they do with their twenty-four hours a day!

Let me give you some idea about the schedule I followed for many years, prior to my semiretirement. There's one thing you could say for me: I did have variety.

My work week started at 6 A.M. on Monday when my wife, Alma, and I got up and fixed our breakfast and had prayer. We had prepared and eaten our breakfast together ever since we were married. We had a cook, but she didn't come till later.

I did not have a chauffeur. I drove my own car and left the house about 7:15 so that I could be at Holiday Inns headquarters by 7:45 for the regular meeting of the executive committee.

The meeting may have lasted two or three hours or may have taken all morning.

After it was over, we had a meeting of the finance committee. We took a look at the figures—the cash we had on hand, the cash we would need for the week, or the next month, and considered where it would come from. We also discussed our commitments in regard to our construction program and what new insurance we would need. We just took a good general look at the cash box.

Then Kemmons Wilson, chairman of the board, and I had a conference in regard to our partnership interests. We had Alodex Corporation and Walkem Development Company, big operations in themselves. Walkem is one of the largest stockholders in Holiday Inns and had other holdings and large real-estate developments. Kemmons and I also owned mineral rights on 24,000 acres in one tract near Alexandria, Louisiana. So we always had matters to talk over just between us, ideas to exchange, in starting the week on Monday. We did this before lunch, if the other meetings hadn't taken all morning. If they ran till noon, then we had a get-together later.

On Monday I usually had lunch with some of the senior officers. I liked to feel their pulse, find out how their blood pressure was, learn if they had any problems they'd like to talk about. It was helpful to them and to me to sit, eat and chat informally.

Immediately after lunch I tried to answer some of the telephone calls that had accumulated during the morning. Then about 2:30 or 3 P.M. Jack Rice, my assistant, came in to see me with a list of items that he thought I should make decisions on. So I studied the list, listened to his explanation of the items and gave him my answers.

Mrs. Ora Wood, my secretary for more than 25 years, came in as soon as Jack left, and she, too, had a list of items requiring my attention. She also told me about people who wanted to see me, some of whom had been waiting for some time in the outer office. And she reminded me of appointments. I saw those who did have appointments and as many of the others as I could work into the schedule.

Before I left the office for the day I signed the letters that Mrs. Wood had waiting for my signature, and I dictated other letters that she would write as she found time. But I rarely finished all the dictation that I should have done, so I took home a batch of letters that had to be answered and also took a list of phone calls that I hadn't been able to get to at the office.

So, at home later in the afternoon, while waiting for the cook to serve dinner to Alma and me, I continued to work. I dictated letters and memos into a machine, and I really gave my phones a workout. I had trained myself to do several things simultaneously. I could, for instance, listen to someone on the phone while reading a letter on another subject, or while writing notes about something else.

I had four unlisted phones, each a different color. Some people had the number of one of my phones but not the numbers of the others. I often could tell by the color of the phone ringing what business associates were calling me and which of my companies was involved.

One of my phones was a WATS (wide area telephone service), and I could sit and make long-distance calls on it all over the United States. I made my calls to the Atlantic seaboard and to other places in the Eastern time zone first. Because of the difference in time, it was an hour later there than it was here. If I waited till after I finished dinner, the people I wanted to reach would have had their dinner and might have been out for the evening. I called at a good time to catch them at home, relaxed, just as I was, when we weren't under pressure.

After I finished my Eastern time-zone calls, I moved to the Central zone, and then on across the country to Rocky Mountain and Pacific Coast time. I made calls to those time zones after we had had our dinner, for it was much earlier out there.

Alma and I went to the den after dinner. I finished my telephoning, and we read the paper. We sometimes watched a short TV program. If I had time, I also read a book and listened to one.

This requires some explaining, doesn't it? I have told you how I could do several things simultaneously. Well, I used that ability in reading books. I employed a young lady with a very pleasing voice to make tape recordings of books I selected. Then, at home in the evening, I listened to those tapes through earphones, and, at the same time, I read another book. I had a notebook and pencil, and when I read or heard something I especially wanted to remember, I stopped the tape, put down the book, and made notes.

In that way I enjoyed two books at one time and got what I wanted out of them. The system was certainly a great timesaver.

Most of the books I read were nonfiction—biography, business, politics, religion.

Since I believed in using every minute to the fullest, I also tried the theory that you can learn while asleep. The idea is that if you go to sleep while listening to a recording, and the recorder continues to play, the information will go into your subconscious mind and will be stored there. You can pull it out into your conscious mind as you need it, provided, of course, you learn how to do the psychological trick.

I recall that once, during the period of my tests, I was making a speech and a very apt quotation from Abraham Lincoln popped into mind. I used it. Later, as I thought about it, I was puzzled. I couldn't remember ever having read it before I used it. Maybe I had heard it while asleep listening to a radio program. In some of my tests I left the radio on all night.

But, other than that, I can't credit the "learning while you sleep" system with any positive result. And it is doubtful that it should be credited with that one incident. Perhaps there is some other explanation for it.

And so, that's the way my week usually went . . . doing the things that I enjoyed doing most in a day that began at 6:30 A.M. and ended at 10:30 P.M. Sure, there were irritations, worries, problems. And, sometimes, there were hurts and disappointments when something I'd done didn't work out in spite of my best efforts or when someone I'd put my confidence in didn't quite come up to my expectations. But, as Dr. Norman Vincent Peale is fond of saying, "The only people that I know without problems are dead folks . . . and, for all I know, some of them may still have problems!"

Saturday was a pleasant day, which I spent mostly at home. Small groups—executives of our companies—came out to the house by appointment, and we sat in comfortable deck chairs around our swimming pool, drank soft drinks and talked. Our pool was in a tropical-like enclosed pavilion with pretty flowers and small trees and was comfortable winter and summer. We discussed ideas and opportunities for Holiday Inns, Medicenters, construction projects, the development of new subdivisions and what not. We usually had a good time, dreaming, planning, "making lemonade," a favorite expression of mine. When an associate reported he had a business lemon on his hands and asked me what to do about it, I said, "Oh, let's just figure out a way to make lemonade of that lemon."

I always tried to get to the barbershop on Saturday, and I also visited my mother, who lived at Rosewood, the first nursing home we built.

Mrs. Johnson and I had dinner together at home on Saturday night, as we did on every other night, and then we read or watched TV. And, of course, I always had some telephone calls to make. We rarely went out to a show or party. We weren't anti-social; just didn't have time for such things. After a furious week we were ready to stay at home on Saturday night. It was the night on which we watched more TV than on any other night.

Sunday we went to church, rested, visited with relatives and friends, attended to urgent matters that couldn't wait.

That's the way my week went, as a rule, but there were plenty of exceptions to the rule. I had to do a lot of traveling in connection with our business—from five thousand to twelve thousand miles a month—and, to save time, I did it in our plane. It was common for me to fly to New York, transact business and get back in time to put in a few more hours before going to bed.

I also did a lot of traveling in connection with extra-curricular activities. I was invited to make speeches at business and church meetings, graduation exercises, prayer breakfasts, conventions of various kinds. I couldn't accept all the invitations I received, but I accepted as many as I could. If I could tell people something that might help them to be better and more successful men and women, I felt it was my duty to do so. In many of my speeches I tried to emphasize what I believe is most important in life—the development of the proper attitude. I mean attitude toward God, family, country, job, your fellow man—a positive, friendly, thankful attitude. The reason many people don't succeed and are unhappy is that they have sour, negative, resentful attitudes.

Well, as I was saying, I did a lot of traveling, so my routine weekly schedule often was disrupted. When it was, I simply had to double up on my office and home work till I caught up.

So that's how I got things done, how I got the most out of each day. No magic, no 1-2-3 formulas, no secrets. There was only one way I knew to get two days' work out of one: work sixteen hours a day.

14

NOT A NURSING HOME,
NOT A HOSPITAL

Some wise man once said that the secret to all business success is "Find a need and fill it." This philosophy has been a key factor in most every venture I've undertaken.

I have told you how the organization of Holiday Inns of America came out of an expensive and unsatisfactory auto trip taken by my partner, Kemmons Wilson. After stopping at dirty, uncomfortable motels and paying unreasonably high prices, Kemmons saw a great opportunity in the motel field.

Now let me give you the background of another fast-growing organization which he and I head and which also came out of a rather negative experience. The name of the organization is Medicenters of America. I am chairman of the board, and he is president.

Today Medicenters are operating and are being built in many cities across America as the outgrowth of a sad and costly experience Mrs. Johnson and I had a few years ago.

A Medicenter is an intermediate-care medical facility about halfway between a hospital and a nursing home.

This multimillion-dollar program started the day in 1953 when we received a telephone call from the operator of a small hotel in Mississippi. My wife's father, Ernest McCool, a widower, was living at the hotel, and he had become ill and needed attention.

Alma and I drove down there, got Mr. McCool and brought him to Memphis. He lived for five years after that, and most of the time he was not sick enough to be in a hospital but was too sick to stay at home, especially since Alma had to go to the office every day—was important to the operation of it—and couldn't stay at home with him. We couldn't find a nursing home that we felt confident would give him all the attention he needed, so we had to keep him in a hospital. That cost us, including nursing care, about $75,000 for the five years he lived.

That experience convinced us that there was a great need for a first-class nursing home in our city, and we determined to build the finest home of that kind to be found in America. We prayed for guidance in doing it.

We hired a perceptive young man and sent him to visit nursing homes all over the country, to study them and pick up ideas, to talk to the operators of the homes, the patients, public-health officials, doctors. We wanted to know what good features to build into our model nursing home and what bad features to avoid, and we wanted to know how to run it after we built it.

Our investigator spent a year traveling, and then we sifted all his reports, called in our architects and discussed design with them and went to work on construction. We built a beautiful building with a 150-bed capacity that cost, equipped, $1,500,000. We named it Rosewood, and we

were mighty proud of it. We felt we had achieved our goal
—that we had built the finest nursing home in America.

But it didn't take us long to see that we had overdone it.
We had made just about every error we could make, despite our careful preparatory research. We overdesigned,
overbuilt and overfinanced it.

Our mistakes, however, didn't kill our enthusiasm over
filling a great need in the nursing-home field. As a matter
of fact, even before Rosewood in Memphis was finished, we
had started another one in Hot Springs, Arkansas.

In building and operating our Rosewoods, we were from
three to five years ahead of the times. They were more like
fine hotels than the depressing nursing homes of that day—
landscaped sites, beautiful buildings, luxurious furnishings
and every comfort and convenience. We had air-conditioning throughout, with individual room control. We provided
both private and semi-private rooms, but no rooms had
more than two beds. All had either full or half-baths. And
each room was equipped with television, radio and an
audio-visual nurses-call system, all controlled from the patient's bed. We had physical therapy and oxygen therapy
facilities and some laboratory facilities. We had recreation
rooms, a chapel, barber and beauty shops, entertainment
programs of various kinds. We had registered nurses on
duty twenty-four hours a day and were fully staffed in all
respects.

We had to charge more than ordinary nursing homes
charged, naturally. But people were reluctant to pay more,
despite the fact that they got so much more for their money,
and acceptance of the new ideas came slowly. Mrs. Johnson and I donated more than $500,000 to Rosewood in
Memphis during the next few years to keep it open. It also
took donations to keep the one in Hot Springs going. But

our desire to provide nursing homes where people could find beauty, peace, comfort and proper care persisted.

We are glad now that we did persist. Our Memphis Rosewood was a pretty big and sour lemon at first, and there were times when we feared we might run out of sugar before we succeeded in making lemonade, but we finally did. And what a refreshing drink it has turned out to be. In view of what it has led to, and in view of the way we have been leaping and swinging ever since, there may be some who think we made something a little more potent than lemonade out of that lemon.

Not only did our experience lead on to the organization of Medicenters of America, but Rosewood itself eventually got out of the red into the black. In fact, it became so popular that we had to enlarge it. We added fifty-five more beds, making it a 203-bed facility.

Our entry into the nursing-home field came to the attention of a man named Stewart Bainum, who had been in the business a number of years. He invited me to come to Washington and discuss the possibility of our entering into a partnership to build nursing homes in the general area of the national capital. I went, liked him, and we made a contract to build and operate five homes. They are at Towson, Wheaton and Hyattsville, Maryland, and at Richmond, Virginia, and Cherry Hill, New Jersey.

My wife and I also built one entirely on our own at Fairhope, Alabama. And in partnership with a Washington lawyer, Herbert S. Colton, we built nursing homes in the Carolinas—Winston-Salem, Spartanburg, Columbia. We also built one in Wilmington, Delaware.

Those homes filled a real need in their communities and turned out to be pretty good investments.

Now, let's go back for a moment to No. 1—Rosewood in Memphis. Friends who inspected it after it was finished were so impressed that they said, "Wallace, how much would it cost you to make this into a complete hospital?" I said, "Oh, man, I don't know." But that started me to thinking, and I had a survey made. We found we could add operating and X-ray rooms and other hospital facilities to our nursing homes and come up with complete hospitals at about 60 percent of the usual cost of hospitals, based on the national average. That was an interesting discovery that kept me thinking about it.

So one day when we had a large nursing home, another Rosewood, under construction in Houston, Texas, I made a sudden decision. There seemed to be more need and more opportunity for sound investment in a hospital there than in a nursing home. So, I told Bobby Hansom, then a vice-president of Wallace E. Johnson Enterprises, to change the plans. He hardly knew what to say. Perhaps we should think about it some more. We would change the nursing home into a general hospital. He is a dynamic young man, used to getting sudden and challenging orders from me, but that order was almost too much for him. He looked shocked, and then his expression turned into one of disbelief. He thought I had to be kidding. Why we already had our two-story nursing home almost completed! The roof was on. Did I really mean I wanted him to tear it off, add another story—operating rooms and all that? Bobby didn't say so, but I could tell he thought I was either off my rocker or somebody had put crazy ideas into my head.

"You can do it," I said. "Go to it."

Bobby, as I say, is a young man who can accept a challenge, no matter how difficult it may seem. He did go to it, and we built Rosewood General Hospital—at a cost of about $14,000 a room, despite the extra cost in changing the plans. And that was an outstanding construction accomplishment, for the national average for hospital construction at that time was $27,000 a room. That was in 1963.

That sudden decision in Houston was one of the biggest and best I ever made. That led to the organization of the Johnson Enterprises Contract Division, to build hospitals, high-rise apartments, big office buildings, etc. Prior to that, we had specialized mostly in home construction. We had learned that we could build such big facilities at greatly reduced costs.

Rosewood Hospital in Houston was built and is operated by its own nonprofit foundation, which, in turn, is sponsored by the Wallace E. Johnson—E. B. McCool Foundation.

Some doctors and others in Indianapolis, Indiana, heard about our accomplishment in Houston and asked us to discuss with them the possibility of building a hospital in their city. We did, and, as a result, we built a 285-bed hospital at from 60 to 70 percent of the average cost of hospitals. We built it as contractors for the Indianapolis group.

It was opened as soon as we completed it. It is in operation now, and the owners are very happy with it.

The success of that project sent us on to St. Louis, where we built a 165-bed hospital, a forty-two-office doctors' building and an extended-care facility for the Christian Hospital. In all it was a $7,000,000 project.

Then we also built a smaller hospital in Farmington, Missouri. And we returned to Houston to construct another one there—Sam Houston Memorial Hospital. It, like the first one, was built and is operated by a nonprofit foundation sponsored by the Wallace E. Johnson—E. B. McCool Foundation. Our reputation for doing the job better and for less money spread in the medical field and, with the tremendous growth of business, we decided to form a new company that would specialize in medical complex development: Medical Development Services, Inc. Under the leadership of Bobby Hansom, MDSI has what we believe to be the finest medical development specialists in the field.

But back to nursing homes. Some friends who knew about our new business asked me if I thought we could build a national chain of nursing homes just as Kemmons Wilson and I had built a chain of Holiday Inns. I studied about it and came to the conclusion that it had possibilities. So one day I sat down with Kemmons and we discussed it. He, too, became interested.

We kicked the idea around in the next few days, and somehow word of what we were thinking about leaked out. We began to get telephone calls from people who said they heard Holiday Inns was going into the nursing-home business, and they wanted to get in on it. And then I got a phone call from a reporter for the *Wall Street Journal* asking about it. I said the report wasn't true, that Holiday Inns wasn't expanding into that field, which, of course, was true. Kemmons and I had not been thinking of nursing homes as Holiday Inns subsidiaries. The homes would be built by a separate corporation we would form. But the *Wall Street Journal* didn't print my interview, and the rumor persisted. And later in the week, the *Journal* reporter called again.

"I understand that Holiday Inns are fixing to go into the franchising of nursing homes," he said, "and I am going to write a story about it, based on the information I have. But I think you should tell us what you are going to do so we can get it straight."

"Wait a minute, wait a minute," I said. "If that's what you are going to do, hold everything till I can get my partner in on this conversation."

I went to Kemmons' office, told him the *Wall Street Journal* was on the phone and asked him to come into my office and get in on the interview. We talked to the reporter for about an hour, and the next day the *Journal* devoted almost a fourth of the front page to a report on our thoughts in regard to the building of a chain of nursing homes across the nation.

After that we really got moving. Since the nursing-home business and the motel business are so different, we, of course, saw that the two should not be combined. We had to have an entirely separate organization and we needed a good name for it. We decided to call the new organization Medicenters of America. John DeCell became president. And right here I'd like to tell you how John happened to be in on our first conference about Medicenters. It is a true story that I have told on John in speeches when he was present, and it was always good for a laugh.

He was a graduate of the University of Mississippi— had majored in statistics, business administration—and had had some experience in hospital administration with the Army. Then he had come to work for Allied Mortgage & Investment Company, now Alodex, Corporation, one of our real-estate corporations. He struck me as a bright young fellow.

One day Kemmons and I needed a statistician for Walkem Development Company, another of our real-estate firms, so we ran a blind ad in the paper. Well, lo and behold, one of the applications we received came from a young man who already was working for us—John DeCell. He wrote a fine letter, telling all about his background and qualifications and explaining that he was fed up with his present position because he didn't like his boss and felt frustrated and didn't think he could get anywhere with the firm.

I sent word for him to come to my office, I had something I wanted to talk to him about. When he walked in, I had his letter on my desk. I picked it up and asked if

he had written it. You can imagine his surprise when he
learned we had run the blind ad he had answered. He was
embarrassed and flustered, scared. He felt he was through
as far as we were concerned, and he had nothing to gain
by backing up. So he stuck to his complaints about his
situation and went into more detail about it. We had a long
talk, and I was favorably impressed by his attitude, his
frankness, his analytical mind. Instead of firing him, I had
him transferred from Allied to the Johnson Enterprises
office and assigned him to investigative work in connection
with our nursing homes. He gave some valuable assistance
in building several homes in the Carolinas.

So when Kemmons and I decided to go into the nursing-home business on a national scale, we naturally thought
of John as a good man to turn loose on the project.

After more study and investigation, our ideas changed.
It seemed to us that there was a greater need of facilities
that would be about halfway between nursing homes and
hospitals than there was need for ordinary nursing homes.
Hospitals everywhere were crowded, and their rates had to
be high—and were getting higher all the time. And one of
the reasons they were crowded was that many patients had
to stay in them through periods of convalescence because
there was no other place for them to go and still get the
special care they needed. Nursing homes couldn't provide
it. But facilities better equipped and staffed could and still
not require the capital investment nor the operating budg-
ets of hospitals. Although the rates of such institutions
would have to be higher than nursing-home rates, they
would be much lower than hospital rates.

We sent John DeCell on a tour to explore the possibilities
of the new idea, to get the opinions of those most concerned with the problems involved. He visited hospitals
and talked with administrators and with doctors and

nurses. He talked with the officers of medical societies, and insurance companies that sell hospital insurance, and he talked with government officials. Medicare was coming into the health picture of the nation and would be intensely interested in the costs of proper nursing.

All of the reaction was favorable, and most of it was enthusiastic. The insurance companies could see how it would save them millions of dollars. It would mean, for instance, that many of their policy-holders would stay in a hospital a week or ten days and then be transferred to a Medicenter for the rest of the period of convalescence— say, three, four or five weeks—instead of spending the whole time in the hospital at high hospital rates. The same thing applied to Medicare patients and would mean great savings to the government.

Doctors also thought well of the idea because they saw it would help to relieve the shortage of hospital beds and make it easier for them to get their patients admitted on short notice and because it would save money without lowering the quality of the service. The doctors also liked our plan to have Medicenters built adjacent to or near hospitals, which would make it convenient for them to continue to visit their patients after they were transferred to the extended-care unit.

So, with John's enthusiastic reports to back up our preliminary thoughts and ideas, we got away from the original plan to build nursing homes. Instead of building homes where the aged would go to finish out their lives, with little or no hope of ever leaving alive, we decided to build beautiful places of comfort and luxury, with private baths, carpets, radio and TV, intercom systems—places where people would enjoy resting and convalescing for a short while and where they would find pleasure in receiving their friends, secure in the realization that competent nurses were on duty at all times, that all the equipment necessary for convalescence was available and that their doctors were nearby.

We had learned a lot about nursing-home construction in building our Rosewoods and the homes in the Washington areas and in the Carolinas, and, after further studies, we found that we could construct and equip beautiful multistoried Medicenters for about $7,500 per bed, plus the cost of the land, as compared to a cost of $35,000 per bed for a general acute hospital, according to the national average.

We also learned that a general hospital, when properly staffed, requires almost three persons—2.62, to be exact—to serve each patient. In Medicenters we found that we would need less than one employee per patient—.75.

So you can see how we could operate Medicenters as private enterprise, pay taxes as other businesses do and still charge approximately half of what general hospitals charge.

15

MY IDEA OF
PUBLIC RELATIONS

Most businessmen today know how important good public relations is, but some, I fear, don't have a broad enough conception of what constitutes public relations. They think the term refers only to their dealings with their customers and with the press, radio and TV. It includes that, all right, but such contacts are just a part of the picture.

To me, everything I do involves public relations—my relations with my fellow executives and with our employees, with our customers, with the press, with the public as a whole, with the people who come to see me or who write me about everything under the sun, and even with our competitors. All such contacts and communications are public relations, in my opinion, and they are all important. They help create the composite image the public has of us and our company.

I don't know of any better guidelines for successful public relations than the Golden Rule and the teachings of

Jesus—sincerity, honesty, friendliness, compassion, kindness, fairness, humility. Anyone who cultivates those traits and strives to be governed by them will not have any serious public-relations problems.

Publicity of various kinds—newspaper, magazine, TV, radio—is, of course, very important. We have an advertising and public-relations department at Holiday Inns headquarters. The department gets out publications and literature for our Innkeepers and employees. They handle our relations with the press, radio and TV, and assist with programs for our people when they come to headquarters from all over for annual meetings and special conferences. They help to entertain VIPs who come to visit us. They write pamphlets and leaflets and handle our advertising.

Our program of religious services, which we are developing on a far-flung scale, is another phase of our public relations.

We initiated a chaplain program at Holiday Inns. The Reverend W. A. Nance, who came to us after having served as pastor of churches for a number of years, became a resident chaplain of Holiday City. He conducted a prayer breakfast for executives every Wednesday, and he arranged for Sunday services at Holiday Inns, not only here but all over the country.

The services were held in Inn meeting rooms, were nondenominational and lasted only thirty minutes. No offering was taken. Local ministers rotated in making talks.

In this way we reach with the Gospel thousands of traveling people who cannot or will not take the time to attend a regular church service on Sunday. We hope that after a few minutes of worship, meditation and prayer they will go on their way in a happy mood, at peace with God and with themselves. And who knows? After reflecting upon the uncertainties of life and the certainty of death, they may drive more carefully. We may help to save lives.

Yes, we think our religious program is an important one.

I am just as concerned about good public relations for Wallace E. Johnson Enterprises as I am about those of Holiday Inns, and I have a public-relations director for my other interests and I cooperate with both the Inns' and Enterprises' public-relations departments by making myself accessible to reporters and cameramen, and I try to give them straightforward, truthful answers to their questions.

You know the old saying, "Honesty is the best policy." I believe that, and it is especially true in public relations.

Newspapermen have good memories. If you lie to them and they catch you in the lie—and the chances are that they will, sooner or later—or if you give them a bum steer, they'll remember it, and forever after there will be a credibility gap between you and them, to your disadvantage.

But I'm aggressive when it comes to public relations. Sometimes, maybe, too aggressive.

One of my wife's favorite stories is about the time we and our friends, the Grady Harrisons, were returning to Memphis from a trip to Arkansas. There was a traffic tie-up on the approach to the bridge over the Mississippi River. Well, Grady and I both like to meet people, so we got out and walked up along the line of cars idling up ahead of us, speaking to people and shaking hands. I stuck out my hand to one fellow, turned on a smile and said, "Howdy, I'm Wallace E. Johnson." He, a little reluctantly, reached out and grasped my hand—and then I saw his hand was all broken out with some kind of terrible rash.

"Gee," he said as I released my grip on his hand, "I sure hope you don't catch what I've got. Had this stuff for years, and just can't get rid of it. Gives me fits."

That, of course, frightened me, and I went back to our car and was absolutely miserable. I wrapped my right hand with my handkerchief so that I wouldn't touch myself or the steering wheel with it and really suffered till I got home and gave my hand a good scrubbing and an antiseptic rinse.

That discouraged me from glad-handing for a while, but in time I resumed it as enthusiastically as ever. I still enjoy walking up to strangers, shaking hands and introducing myself. You can win a lot of new business that way and sometimes make enjoyable friendships.

I am equally aggressive when it comes to good public relations with our stockholders. When I prepare to leave on a trip, I have my secretary get me up a list of stock-holders in the area I am to visit. I want to know how much stock they own, when they bought it and how much they paid for it, and I also want their addresses and telephone numbers. We have telephone directories of other cities, and she can look up the numbers.

I take the list with me, and when I have a few spare minutes I call stockholders on the phone. I say: "Hello. . . . this is Wallace E. Johnson. You own twenty-five shares in our company [or whatever the number may be] which you bought on such and such a date, and for which you paid so much [and I give the exact amount]. I am in town for a few hours, and just thought I'd call and give you a report on your company."

And I tell him how we are expanding, how business is, the present value of his stock and invite questions. I pass a few pleasantries and ask how everything is with him and his family.

Some think the call is from a joker, at first. When I convince them that I really am one of the officers of Holiday Inns, they are pleased. Convincing them isn't too difficult, for no practical joker would have so much information about their stock and about Holiday Inns.

Sometimes when I am traveling I stop at Holiday Inns without having made a reservation or having given any notice of my coming. I walk up to the desk and register as any other guest would, and the clerk may not recognize either me or my name. I get a kick out of it when that happens. It gives me a chance to size up their attitude toward the public and the service they give. It gives me a chance to check on other things, too. We have porters at Holiday Inns, for instance, who are available to help people with their baggage if they want help. But we have a rule that porters must not buzz around guests, insisting on helping them in order to get tips. That's annoying. So when I go into a Holiday Inn and am not expected or recognized, I have an opportunity to check on that rule. I think it is a good one.

I might add, though, that I never register under an assumed name and never try to mislead anyone as to my identity. I am there as a guest, not as a spy.

I don't suppose there is a company anywhere in the world that isn't in favor of courtesy on the part of its employees in dealing with the public. Courtesy is like mother, home and apple pie. Everybody is for it. But it is one thing to be perfunctorily for something and quite another thing to be enthusiastically and actively for it. We at Holiday Inns make it an important part of our everday operation. We know that courtesy is something that requires no capital investment, but which pays great dividends. We realize our success depends on it. So we demand it of all employees, and we try to teach it by both precept and example.

Our training courses include instruction in courtesy, and we issue pamphlets giving employees suggestions.

We remind them that the guest is the most important person in our business and that we aren't doing him a favor by renting him a room, selling him a meal, helping him get various kinds of information. The guest isn't obligated to us. We are obligated to him. He isn't to be looked upon as a room number but as a human being with feelings, emotions, problems. We impress upon our employees that the guest is the fellow who makes it possible for them to have jobs.

So we encourage our employees to learn the names of our guests, to smile and speak to them and to try to be helpful in any way they can. And we require our employees, especially the Innkeepers and front-desk men and women, to be animated encyclopedias of information about their areas. They must be ready to answer all kinds of questions—know the locations of churches and the hours of service, recommend scenic spots and things of historical interest worth seeing, tell guests where golf courses and tennis courts are and how to get to them, direct them to fishing and hunting places, theaters, stores, the chamber of commerce, post office. Our employees must be able to give up-to-date information on the cultural life of their areas, the colleges and schools, and about the industries, the population.

And, of course, they must know the answers to questions involving little personal needs—where to buy an out-of-town newspaper, find a barbershop or beauty parlor, get a pair of shoestrings.

During the first years of Holiday Inns, Kemmons and I

used to be present for ground-breaking ceremonies when construction of a new Inn was started. We considered that good public relations. It got us helpful publicity. And later, we'd go back for dedication ceremonies when the Inn was opened. We got a great kick out of it.

We would still enjoy doing that, but it no longer is possible. We just can't do it and carry on our work. New Inns open every week. We have averaged over two new Inns a week since 1962. One week we opened twelve new ones. The total is now well over 1,700.

There are Holiday Inns that I have never seen!

You can be sure, though, that we saw them on the drawing boards before and during their construction and approved the sites and plans. And you can be sure that we keep up with the way they are doing by studying reports on them.

In front of every Holiday Inn is our Great Sign. On it is a special-events panel, which we use as a theater uses marquee panels. We change the signs every day or two, using attractive sets of movable letters of the alphabet. We advertise meetings being held at our Inns, welcome distinguished guests or touring parties, offer special dishes being served in our restaurants, arouse interest in something unusual we are doing, make humorous cracks.

Our signs attract lots of attention and create good will. Even actors and actresses who are used to seeing their names up in lights get a kick out of being welcomed on our great sign.

These things are all a part of public relations, and they are all important. There are other phases of it, for, as I said at the beginning, I consider everything that I do that involves contact or communication with other people as public relations. My speech-making comes under that head.

Why, even some of the private little speeches I make to

my wife can be classed as public relations—when I am trying to sell her on a business venture that she is skeptical about.

Alma is a great public-relations representative. She's had lots of practice. One day her diplomatic handling of a complaint may have saved me a sock in the eye.

She was at the front desk at Johnson Enterprises, and I was seated at a table nearby, working on some papers, when an angry customer came in. He was steaming. She asked him what she could do for him, and he said he was looking for that Wallace E. Johnson. He had bought one of our houses, and he had complaints about it. Just let him at that Wallace E. Johnson and he'd get satisfaction or take it out of Johnson's hide.

Alma didn't call me, didn't even look in my direction. She just let him blow off steam and made a note of his complaints. I sat there with my ears cocked, listening to it all and not saying a word. I, too, have pretty good judgment sometimes. That big fellow was not a man to confront at the moment.

After he left, Alma turned to me and said, "All right, Big Shot. What have you got to say?"

"I say we fix his house. Otherwise, you may have to fix me."

16

SOME PAIN,
SOME PLEASURE

As I point out repeatedly, the Bible has been a great inspiration and help to me throughout my whole life. In times of sorrow, disappointment and discouragement, I have found Romans 8:28 of special comfort. I like to keep it in mind and like to quote it. It reads: "And we know that all things work together for good to them that love God, to them who are the called according to his purpose."

Life's problems sometimes put a strain on one's faith, but that passage of the Scripture enabled Alma and me to bear them. It was certainly a great help when we lost our only child.

The baby was born to us years ago, when we were a young couple. We were happy at the prospect of becoming parents. The months of anticipation were thrilling ones.

The baby was born at home, as so many babies were in those days, especially in small towns. It was a very difficult labor for Alma. The baby made a breech presentation, and the doctor had to use instruments. In doing so he bruised the head. It was a girl, and immediately after birth a large blisterlike swelling formed. We had already decided on the name Nancy Jo, in case we had a girl.

Little Nancy Jo's condition was critical from the very start, due to her head injury, and the next day the doctor decided that an emergency operation was necessary to relieve the swelling and pressure. He was preparing to perform it in our living room when she died, having lived only thirty-six hours.

Alma was in a serious condition—was very ill—and for a while it looked as if we might lose her, too. It was a period of great strain and anguish, and we needed all the faith we could muster to sustain us. But God did sustain us and we came through the tragedy still believing in His eternal wisdom and goodness. It was hard to become reconciled to the loss of our baby, but we found comfort in the passage I have quoted: "And we know that all things work together for good to them that love God, to those who are the called according to his purpose."

Little Nancy Jo was the only child born to us. It has been a great disappointment, of course, that no others have come to bless our union, which otherwise has been perfect and complete. We cannot understand why our only one should have been taken from us—and taken so soon. But we do not question God's goodness and love. We have continued to have faith.

Although we haven't any children of our own, we have found pleasure in the children of others and have been of help to many of them in our church, charity and philanthropic activities. And, of course, we are very proud of our nieces, Janice and Alma Elizabeth, daughters of Alma's brother and his wife, and feel that they are our very own. They have given us a lot of pleasure and have helped to fill what otherwise might have been a void in our lives.

In fact, when Alma Elizabeth was born, I was probably the most excited man in Memphis and made a mistake that the family still laughs about. I was a lot more excited than Barney McCool, the baby's father, for he wasn't in town and didn't know what was going on.

The baby, you see, came two months prematurely, and Barney was away on a business trip. His home and our home are on adjoining lots, and when his wife, Ines, felt labor pains she called to us for help. Alma and I rushed over to the McCool home. I called an ambulance but didn't wait for it to arrive. I'd go on ahead and make all the necessary arrangements at the hospital—alert the obstetrical department, get a room and all that. Alma would ride in the ambulance with Ines. And, of course, Ines's doctor was called. He said he'd meet us at the hospital.

I'm afraid I did a little speeding in getting to Baptist Hospital. I spread the big news, signed up for a room and paced the floor.

Then a happy thought struck me. There was a florist's shop nearby. I ran to it and bought some flowers and placed them in the room I had engaged. I hadn't been so excited in a long time.

Minutes seemed like hours as I nervously walked around —and wondered what in the world had happened to Ines, Alma and the ambulance. I went down to the Emergency Department entrance. Had an ambulance come with a maternity patient? They said, no, not during the past hour.

A great fear gripped me. Maybe the ambulance had had a wreck. Perspiration popped out on me. I fidgeted and stewed around.

Finally, I got on the phone and did some frantic checking—and learned what a blunder I had made. Ines's doctor practiced at Methodist Hospital, and they had gone there, naturally. And congratulations! I had become the uncle of a beautiful baby girl.

I was the guy who did the pacing on that birth, not Barney.

But I was telling you what great help Romans 8:28 has been to me. I can recall another instance when it was of great comfort.

One day in November 1966 Dr. James F. Eaves and I took off in a helicopter from the campus of Baptist Theological Seminary in New Orleans. He was pastor of Union Avenue Baptist Church in Memphis, where I have been a member for years, and we were on the board of the Seminary. I also was president of its development board. So we had been there for a meeting, and we engaged the helicopter to fly us to the airport, as we were pressed for time.

When we were up about 150 feet, the engine conked out—and down we plunged, clipping power lines. Dr. Eaves was seated behind me, and he grabbed my head and held it down. We hit with a mighty crash. The gas tank burst but did not explode. The helicopter was a wreck, even though it had rubber pontoons on the landing gear that helped to cushion the shock somewhat.

As we hit, I thought surely it was the end. But, luckily, all three of us were able to walk away from the wreck, although we were hurt and badly shaken up. I had cuts and bruises and several fractured ribs. Dr. Eaves and the pilot also had injuries, but they got off a little lighter than I did.

It was a painful and unnerving experience, and for a few minutes I fear my faith in Romans 8:28 was shaken. How could an accident like that work for anybody's good?

I'll tell you. If I get to worrying about something, I stop and remind myself of that close brush with death. "Why should I be worrying about this thing that I think is so important?" I ask myself. "Man, you are lucky to be alive! You should be thankful that you are here to deal with it."

That relaxes me, and the problem becomes an interesting challenge—an opportunity.

Perhaps it would be a good thing if everybody had at least one close call. It gives you a more healthful attitude toward life.

My belief that all things work together for good to those who love God and are the called according to His purpose sustains me in many situations, as, for instance, when I am subjected to painful criticism.

As I have explained in an early chapter, I am a teetotaler. It is part of my religious faith, and I am sure I am better off without alcohol in my bloodstream and in my mind.

In view of my religious background and connections— I am active in national interdenominational organizations such as the Laymen's National Bible Committee, Religious Heritage of America, the Foundation of Christian Living, Billy Graham Crusades, and Campus Crusade for Christ— I have been criticized in some circles because liquor is sold in the lounges and dining rooms of some Holiday Inns around the world. Some of this criticism has been bitter.

Now, if the matter were left to me alone to decide, I would not let alcoholic beverages be sold in our Inns. But the matter is not left to me. We are a tremendous organization in size. There are other high officers and there are directors. We try to operate in a democratic manner, and they, too, have a vote on such questions. And they think that we must meet competition, that if we don't give people what they want and are willing to pay for, they will go somewhere else. There is no getting around the fact that many do want a drink after a hard day on the road, as an appetizer, or for social reasons at little parties or conferences.

Anyway, the simple fact is that I am outvoted in our organization on this question of liquor. I must either go along with our board or I must sell my stock and get out. And I don't want to do that. I am participating in many worthwhile activities and projects, which are doing much to make life better and happier for thousands of people, and I do not want to cut myself off from this opportunity for service. It isn't the money I make as an officer of Holiday Inns that holds me. I don't need it. My income from my many other enterprises is far more than sufficient for Alma and me.

I used to try to explain my awkward position in regard to liquor in Holiday Inns, but it didn't seem to make my critics any more understanding or tolerant. It is hard to change people's opinions that involve strong convictions of long standing, based on moral and religious beliefs. I give them credit for sincerity, but I don't try to explain anymore. It is one of those things I have to live with.

Alma likes to tell what she calls "the wine-keg story" on me. People who hear it think it's even funnier because I am a teetotaler, but nonetheless played a part in it.

Back in prohibition days, when I was a young fellow managing a lumberyard at Itta Bena, Mississippi, it was rather common practice for businessmen to buy kegs of California grape juice in the fall. They'd put the kegs in storage, pull the bungs so the air could get into them, and in time the grape juice would ferment. They'd have wine to give friends and customers for Christmas.

Well, the owner of the lumberyard got a keg of grape juice and asked me to store it in a corner of an upstairs room. I pulled the bung as he ordered, locked the door and left.

One day some weeks later, as Christmas approached, three of my men were missing from the yard. I looked everywhere for them and finally found them upstairs, passed out, dead drunk!

Somehow they had taken note of the position of the keg and had found a knothole in the wall right near it. They had taken the hose of a fountain syringe and had threaded it through the knothole and into the open bunghole of the keg. They had siphoned out and drunk wine till they had passed out.

Needless to say, our customers didn't get any bottles of wine that Christmas.

On the subject of money, I must admit that I have been very fortunate and have much for which to be thankful and happy. But I have always been happy. Alma and I were happy when I was working for a small salary and we were barely getting by.

We were talking about this recently, and we agreed that we are no happier now than we were when we were in meager circumstances.

Our happiness has never been dependent on money. Happiness comes from within, from the right attitude toward God and toward one another, from work that you enjoy doing, from having worthwhile goals and striving toward them, from helping people and good causes all along the way.

I think a man's success can be measured in two ways: 1. Did he enjoy his work? 2. Did he leave the world a little better place than he found it?

Any man who can give a positive answer to those two questions is a success, no matter whether he has ten dollars or ten million.

Oh, it's nice to have money. I enjoy making it, and I

enjoy giving it away. Money was made to do good with. I have always said money is like fertilizer. You should spread it all around and make things grow.

Here's something else about money that many people may not think about: It imposes a heavy responsibility. My wife and I not only thank God constantly for giving us the wisdom to make money, but we also pray earnestly for the wisdom to use it properly. And that's what we strive to do, largely through the Wallace E. Johnson–E. B. McCool Foundation. E. B. McCool, or Barney as he is known to us, is Mrs. Johnson's brother and has been a partner in most of our enterprises.

But getting back to the responsibility of wealth, I often feel the weight of it in making decisions of great importance to the future success of our businesses. Wrong decisions can result in trouble for our enterprises, and that could mean loss of jobs for hundreds of people. I feel my responsibility to them. To have wealth and to be in a top administrative position brings prestige and certain kinds of freedom, but it also can bring a certain kind of enslavement. A man can get caught in a situation where he can't think of only his own desires—not in good conscience.

Then why do I keep driving myself if I don't need the money and if I am convinced that money doesn't bring happiness? My partner, Kemmons Wilson, and I have fun working. We are playing a big, exciting game, seeing how much we can accomplish in an honest, substantial way.

A reporter once asked Kemmons if money was the thing that kept driving him.

"Money is the most unimportant thing in the world," Kemmons said, "if you have enough to live the way you want to live. Anything above that is just something to get out and work with for the fun of doing something."

That expresses my attitude, too.

You know, I find it just about impossible to take a vacation, in the usual meaning of the word. Nobody wants a vacation from pleasure.

The average person's idea of a vacation is to get away from his usual pursuits and do something different for a couple of weeks or a month and perhaps travel. That will get some variety in his life.

But I get all the variety I need, do all the traveling I want, and have all the fun I can stand in my everyday work. So why take a vacation seeking what I already have?

As for taking time off to lie around and rest and do nothing—my, that would be misery. That would kill me. That wouldn't be a vacation. No matter where I went, I'd soon be scouting around for new business opportunities.

Alma used to try to make me take vacations. Once we planned to have a long holiday at Sarasota, Florida, and she read the riot act to me. If I didn't promise to forget business, and if I didn't promise not to go looking around for land to buy, she wasn't going. And that's all there was to it.

I said O.K., I would try to forget business. And off we went. I was determined to humor her and take a vacation. Maybe it would be good for me.

But after we had been there three or four days, doing nothing in particular, I began to get restless. And when a real-estate man heard I was there, called me on the phone and asked if I'd like to look at some property, I was eager to go. I slipped away from Alma on some pretext or other and had an exciting afternoon looking at land. And when I went back to the motel I was all worked up over it and started pacing the floor, thinking about it.

Alma knew me well enough to know that something was up.

"Well," she said in an accusing tone, "what have you bought?"

"I—I haven't bought anything," I said.

"Then what are you thinking of buying?" she persisted. "Come, come. I can tell by the way you're acting that you are thinking of buying something."

I couldn't avoid the issue. I had to confess that the temptation had been just too much for me.

I bought the land, and it turned out to be a happy vacation. Alma forgave me and caught some of my excitement over the deal.

But that's an illustration of the way my vacations usually turned out when I tried to take them. We now go on lots of trips and have a good time, but we don't call them vacations. They are just more of the same.

So, I repeat, the principal reason I drive myself constantly isn't to make money, but to express myself and enjoy life. And that also applies to my thrift. I hate waste in any form. I don't mind admitting that I like to save every dime I can, whether I'm spending the company's money or my own. In my early life I had to watch my nickels in order to get by, and I formed habits of thrift that I can't get rid of—and don't really want to.

I get the best price I can on every contract I make, everything I buy. And I insist on my key men doing the same. But I also tell them that I never want them to drive such a hard bargain that they will seriously hurt the other fellow. I just don't want him to make too big a profit on me.

Speaking of deals, some people have the idea that I buy land anonymously through agents. They think I maneuver that way because I fear the sellers may up the price if they learn they are dealing with a millionaire. Well, they are wrong. I do not hesitate to reveal my identity. I like to look a seller in the eye and dicker with him personally. If he tries to up the price on me, he just cuts himself out of a sale. If I don't think the price is right, I simply do not buy.

As for transactions involving only my personal needs, let me give you an illustration of how I will go to some trouble to save a dollar or two.

We wanted to surround our enclosed swimming pool with tropical plants, to make it a warm little beauty spot even in winter. We learned that to order the plants and have them trucked to Memphis from Florida would cost considerable money. So, on my next business trip down there, I bought the potted plants, rented a trailer and hooked it to my Cadillac and brought the plants back with me. I saved a bit of money.

Now, it may strike some that it was below the dignity of a man in my position to do a thing like that. I do not think that honest work and thrift are below the dignity of any man. I wish a lot of big shots in government felt this way about it, too.

While we are on the subject of money I suppose I should tell you about my old "borrowing hat." It used to inspire a lot of wisecracks among my associates.

It is a battered old felt hat, and for years I wore it every time I went to the bank to borrow money. And since I usually got the loans, we all started looking on that old hat as a sort of luck piece, and that's why I started calling it my borrowing hat. It was all in fun. It never developed into a superstition, as some ball players develop superstitions about their old caps or shoes, but somehow it did give me a little extra confidence as I went to the bank. And when you come right down to it, perhaps that crumpled old hat did create a favorable impression on the bankers. An old hat does somehow suggest hard work, thrift and rugged honesty—that is, when it is worn by a man known to be a responsible citizen.

I wore my borrowing hat for years. I still have it, but don't use it in going to the bank to ask for loans anymore. In fact, I have just about quit wearing a hat. But I frequently still wear apparel that suggests economy and rugged individuality. I sometimes have holes in my shoes, and they show when I cross my legs. This may not help me with the big bankers, but it certainly doesn't seem to handicap me.

But don't get the idea that my wearing shoes with holes in them is an affectation. I find old shoes comfortable, and I develop an affection for them. I hate to part with them long enough to get them repaired. A man whose feet hurt just isn't at his best, no matter whether he's trying to put over a business deal or is courting a girl.

17

MY LEMONADE
PARTNER

I already have told you how my partner, Kemmons Wilson, and I teamed up in 1953 to found Holiday Inns of America and how we have worked in complete harmony since then to build the world's largest motel-hotel chain. Since we no longer are confined to America, but now circle the globe, we have changed the name to Holiday Inns, Incorporated.

I do not feel that this book would be complete if I didn't tell you more about him. Our stories are so entwined that you can't tell one without telling the other.

A newspaperman once interviewed Kemmons and me separately, but he asked both of us some of the same questions. One question was: "What do you consider your biggest piece of luck as a businessman?" and each of us, unbeknown to the other, gave the same answer.

"I think my luckiest break came when Kemmons Wilson asked me to be his partner in developing Holiday Inns," I said.

"My biggest piece of luck was that Wallace Johnson agreed to come in with me," Kemmons answered.

That shows you how Kemmons and I feel about each other. Those were honest answers, given without any collusion whatever.

Speaking of our teaming up, we still get a laugh out of what the late Jimmy Ross, president of the National Bank of Commerce, said when we told him we had formed a partnership and what we had in mind.

"Well," he said, laughing, "I've heard of men joining their assets to form a partnership, but this is the first time I have heard of two fellows joining their liabilities."

He was kidding us, of course, but there was some truth in his joke.

I think one of the main reasons Kemmons and I get along so well is that we speak the same language, have similar backgrounds and the same outlook on life and dream the same dreams. We were both poor boys who grew up making our own way, working hard and long hours. Habits and ambitions formed as mere boys have become our way of life. We don't know any other way. We are both happiest when we are working. Work is Kemmons' play, just as it is mine.

Since we teamed up to build Holiday Inns, we also have teamed up to form and promote other organizations and projects—Medicenters of America, large real-estate and development companies, construction firms, the purchase of big tracts of land to be held for future development.

When we confer to consider a problem, a new deal, to reach a decision in regard to some matter, urgent or otherwise, we often are in complete agreement from the very start. Occasionally, however, we disagree at the beginning. But we never have heated arguments. We never get mad, pound the table and say it has got to be this way, or else.

We have respect for each other's opinion and complete confidence in each other's honesty. So we listen to each other. In that way we get a better and more complete picture of the whole matter than we had at the start. We see aspects that we had not thought of.

If one is not able to win the other over to his viewpoint, then we reach a friendly compromise. And when we reach a decision, it is never Kemmons' decision nor Wallace's. It is *our* decision.

And if it turns out to be a bum one, neither points an accusing finger at the other and says, "I was afraid of that. If you had listened to me in the first place—"

No, when we do make a bad decision, we just shrug or laugh it off—and determine to profit by it. We take our lemon and try to make lemonade. And my partner is one of the best lemonade makers I have ever known.

When I think of how Kemmons and I sit down together in a spirit of friendship and complete confidence in each other and work out our common problems in a give-and-take manner, I have hope for the future of our country and for the whole world, too. Maybe some day large groups —representatives of capital and labor, for instance, or the representatives of minority and majority racial groups, or even the representatives of whole nations—can sit down in the same spirit and settle big issues in harmony.

The key to our relationship is that we don't criticize each other. I never find fault with a decision Kemmons has made in my absence, and he never finds fault with one I have made. We back each other up 100 percent.

When I was absent in Europe, Kemmons made several big real-estate deals involving our partnership, not Holiday Inns. He told me about them upon my return.

"I'll get up all the figures for you," he said. "You can

study them and decide whether you want in on the deals. If not, I'll take them by myself."

"I don't need the figures," I said. "I want in on the deals."

They involved big money, but Kemmons' judgment was good enough for me.

But let me give you a more specific illustration of the confidence we have in each other, even when speed and snap judgment are necessary. This is one of my favorite stories.

Kemmons and his wife, Dorothy, went to Florida on a combination business and pleasure trip. He attended a convention, and then they toured around on a holiday. They had been wanting to see Marineland at St. Augustine, so they went to see it. They stopped for lunch at a restaurant near there. They were wearing sports clothes—Kemmons had on shorts and a shirt open at the neck—and they were relaxed and were enjoying themselves. But Kemmons is like me in that he can never get entirely away from business. He's always looking for an opportunity to make a good deal, to buy something else. That's his idea of fun, too.

Well, Kemmons is full of nervous energy, and he's a fast eater. And he gets fidgety when he has to sit and wait on others to finish. So he got through his lunch in quick time and told Dorothy he'd step up front and talk to the manager a few minutes while she ate her dessert. Kemmons likes to meet people.

"How are land values around here?" he asked the manager.

"Pretty high and getting higher," the manager said. "Step over here to the window with me, and I'll show you something." And they went to the window.

"See those lots over yonder," the manager continued, pointing. "They sold recently for twenty dollars a front foot. But, say, if you are interested in learning more about land prices, you might attend a lot auction being held down the road—some pretty ocean-front stuff. It's starting just about now."

Kemmons got excited. He asked the manager for directions to the tract—right down Highway A-1-A—and he ran back into the café to get Dorothy. She hadn't finished her lunch, but he grabbed her by the hand and said never mind the pie, they had to get going. No time to lose.

Well, she's used to Kemmons. She knew he hadn't suddenly gone crazy. That could mean only one thing—he was hot after a big deal. She snatched up her purse and they left on the run. They jumped into their car, and away they went.

The site of the auction was on an unimproved road that ran from the highway to the beach. The auction was already in progress when they arrived. Several hundred people were gathered around the auctioneer, some real bidders, and some just there out of curiosity. Kemmons was struck by the beauty of the ocean front and began to see visions. He learned the lots were one hundred feet wide, varying in depth, extending all the way between the highway and the ocean.

He also quickly learned about the rules of the auction. A successful bidder had the privilege of buying one or more lots at the same price he paid for the first lot.

Four lots had been sold when Kemmons went into action —two lots in the center had been knocked down for forty dollars a foot. Two less desirable lots at the north end of the property had gone for $22.50 a foot.

The fifth lot put up for sale opened at sixteen dollars, and Kemmons bid seventeen dollars. Someone said eighteen dollars, and someone else shouted nineteen dollars.

Then Kemmons raised it to twenty dollars. There was a pause, and the auctioneer said "Sold!"

"O.K.," the auctioneer said to Kemmons. "Now, would you like to buy another lot at the same price?"

"Why, yes," Kemmons said. "In fact, I'll take 'em all."

The auctioneer looked at Kemmons in astonishment and bidders nudged one another and smiled. They thought it was just an act, that Kemmons was a shill. It was just a little monkey business to stimulate bidding. But the auctioneer knew it wasn't a joke. He had never seen Kemmons before, and he was puzzled. Was the fellow serious? Or was he off his rocker?

"Do you realize we have unsold lots totaling thirty-one hundred feet of frontage?" he asked Kemmons.

"No, I didn't know that," Kemmons said, "but I'll still take it all."

Then the auctioneer was sure he had some kind of nut to deal with. He cut his eyes at Kemmons standing there in shorts and looking like an overgrown Boy Scout and smiled indulgently. "Do you have sixty-two thousand dollars?" he asked.

"Well, I don't have it with me," Kemmons said. "But if you'll get into my car and direct me to the nearest bank, I think I can make arrangements to get it."

The auctioneer questioned Kemmons further, learned who he was and became convinced that the offer was on the up and up. He announced to the crowd that all the lots had been sold, and the auction was over. He went with Kemmons to a local bank, and Kemmons made a call to his Memphis bankers and closed the deal.

That night he called me on the phone and told me what he had done.

"I had to act fast, Partner," he said, "but I think it is a good buy. If you want to come in on it, that's fine. If not, I'll just keep it all."

"Partner," I said, "I want in on it with you."

Title to the property is now held by Medicenters of America, which Kemmons and I head. The value of it is far more than we paid for it.

As I have said, Kemmons and I were both poor country boys, and some people point to us as examples of what can be done under our system of free American enterprise. Sometimes I get the impression they mean that if two dumb guys like us can make a success, anybody can. Well, we don't claim to be geniuses.

Let me tell you about one project that did not turn out so well for us. Alodex was the name of a corporation Kemmons and I formed to build homes and commercial buildings and to develop large suburban tracts such as Southaven, Mississippi. We built a beautiful four-story building at Southaven for our headquarters. Southaven, a pretty little city with a population of about 10,000, adjoins Memphis to the south at the Mississippi-Tennessee line. We played the major and important part in building it. We had the idea and developed it. We are proud of Southaven and the people who live there.

However, affairs became muddled with the Alodex investment and we had to step in and take strong measures to try to save the company. Kemmons and I felt our good names were at stake. Although we were not obligated personally for deficits and losses, we did feel a moral obligation to do what we could financially. Our reputations were involved.

But enough of this. Let's get back to the story of my lemonade partner.

Kemmons was born in Osceola, Arkansas, in 1913. But my sandy-haired, sun-tanned, medium-sized, smiling partner doesn't look that old. Perhaps the reason he looks younger is that he still has a boyish enthusiasm about everything.

He goes at a furious pace about eighteen hours a day, but never seems to be in a hurry. While on the way to an important meeting, he will take time to stop and exchange jokes with a loafer.

His favorite sport is tennis, and he plays it furiously several times a week when he is home. Golf? That's too slow for Kemmons. He wants action and plenty of it.

Kemmons' father died when Kemmons was just a baby, only nine months old. His mother, Mrs. Ruby Lloyd Wilson, moved to Memphis and went to work as a receptionist and assistant in a dentist's office, at eleven dollars a week, to support herself and her baby. She took other part-time work to make ends meet.

Kemmons, as a child, worked at any little jobs he could find that would pay him a nickel or a dime. When he was nine, he got a paper route.

At fourteen Kemmons became a delivery boy for a drugstore. One day while making a delivery to the home of Bill Terry, a famous baseball player, he was hit by a car on Union Avenue. He suffered a compound fracture of his right leg, and it was in a cast for about a year. Medical bills mounted, and Mrs. Wilson had to work harder than ever to pay their debts.

When he was about 17, Kemmons went into business for himself. Even as a boy he had a keen eye for an opportunity. It struck him that people, particularly youngsters, would enjoy popcorn with their movies. Nearly every movie house today sells popcorn, but in those days in 1930–31 the theater popcorn business wasn't very well developed. So Kemmons found a secondhand popper for sale at fifty dollars. He didn't have the money, but he had a glib tongue. He talked the owner into selling him the machine on credit, one dollar a week and nothing down.

Then he rented space in front of a theater for $2.50 a week. The Depression was on, and the theater manager was glad to pick up a few extra dollars wherever he could.

Kemmons worked his popper afternoons and nights, after school and on weekends and holidays and did a good business. He built it up to where he was making thirty dollars a week. That was good money in those dark days, even for adults. In fact, it got so Kemmons was making more money than the manager of the theater, so the manager threw him out. He would go into the popcorn business himself.

Kemmons was out in the cold. No other good location was available at the time, so he sold the theater manager his popcorn machine for fifty dollars. He thus got back all of his invested capital.

He took the money and bought five secondhand pinball machines for ten dollars each and put them in drugstores and cafés. He saved some of his take and bought more machines.

In those days his mother had a clerical job with a large company, and with her salary and Kemmons' income from his machines, they got along comfortably. But when his mother got let out along with others in an economy move, they soon were in a jam. Kemmons had to quit high school in his senior year and go to work full time.

By hustling day and night, he built up his pinball-machine spots and added jukeboxes. He saved every nickel he could, and in time had a small fortune in the bank— $1,700! He decided to use it in building a home for himself and his mother. In those Depression days you could buy residential lots for a song and could name your own price in hiring carpenters, bricklayers, plumbers. Kemmons bought a lot and superintended the building of their little home, although he didn't know anything about construction. But he knew how to pick a good carpenter. Lumber cost him only ten dollars a thousand.

Some months after they moved in, Kemmons got on fire

to expand his business in a hurry. He talked a banker into lending him three thousand dollars on his home. With the new capital he bought more pinball machines and juke-boxes and added cigarette-vending machines to his line.

A year or so later he got a chance to sell their home for $6,500, and he accepted the offer. That big profit got him steamed up. Boy, he was in the wrong business, monkeying with those small-change machines. The homebuilding field was for him.

He built a house next door to the first one, sold it at a profit of two thousand dollars. Then he built others. He was on his way.

He was the busiest young businessman in the Mid-South, for he kept on checking his pinball and other machines while he bought materials, hired workmen and built houses.

In the late Thirties Kemmons began investing in apartment houses which insurance companies had taken at fore-closures and which they were anxious to unload. You could buy them with a down payment of only 10 percent. Kemmons went for them and started pyramiding. When the war broke out, he was the owner of a tremendous amount of such properties, but he owed a million dollars on them.

Kemmons is a patriot, loves our country, and he couldn't stay out of uniform. But as he contemplated going into service and thought of the possibility that he might not return alive, he became frightened. He couldn't leave his mother and wife a million dollars in debt. So he decided to liquidate all his assets, pay off his debts. When he wound it all up, he had about $250,000 in cash to leave them.

And off he went to war with a freer mind. He became a pilot in the Air Transport Command. He flew all over this country at first, and then was transferred to India.

He came out of the war O.K. and full of enthusiasm to get back into the home-construction and real-estate business. And he has been in it, and in various other fields, on a constantly expanding scale ever since—motels and hotels, manufacturing, theaters, all kinds of construction, merchandising, insurance.

In all of his ventures, from the purchase of the fifty-dollar secondhand popcorn machine to his multimillion-dollar deals, Kemmons' mother was his partner—and I mean partner in the real sense of the word—right on up to the day of her death several years ago. She was a lovely, jolly, inspiring woman, always ready to encourage and comfort us, according to our needs, and was a great help in the days when we were struggling to get Holiday Inns on the move, just as my wife Alma was. Mrs. Wilson was a vice-president of Holiday Inns and a real one. She had an office and was on the job every day. Everybody loved and respected her, and she was known affectionately to all of us as Doll.

And of course, Kemmons' lovely wife, the former Dorothy Lee, has been a big help and inspiration to him. She is the perfect, understanding wife and helpmate. If Kemmons has to leave on thirty minutes notice on a trip to Europe, she understands and cheerfully packs his bags. If he brings home four strangers to dinner on short notice, or no notice at all, she doesn't get angry and flustered. If he eats in a hurry and rushes away for an evening conference, she smiles as she sends him on his way.

Kemmons and Dorothy were married at Galloway Methodist Church in Memphis on December 2, 1941—just before he entered World War II. They have five children, now all grown.

I am proud to be the partner of Kemmons Wilson. Although I am twelve years older than he, I never try to pull any seniority on him. In fact, often I feel very humble in his presence and as I see him in action. Kemmons is one of the giants of the world today and was so recognized by the *Sunday Times Magazine*, London, England. In September 1969 they selected "the 1,000 Makers of the 20th Century," men of all nations around the world who have made great contributions to the progress of civilization. Kemmons was in the honored list. He was also the featured subject of a TIME magazine cover story in the June 12, 1972, issue. The picture of Kemmons on the TIME cover is one of my favorites. It seems to capture my partner's happy, youthful exuberance.

In May 1968 he was the commencement speaker at the University of Alabama, at which time the school conferred on him an honorary Doctor of Laws degree. In that speech he said: "There is no substitute for hard work—even today. As long as we're willing to work, the American dream is not dead. It is alive and thriving. I believe freedom to work is second only to our religious freedom."

And to that I say, "Amen, Partner!"

In another speech Kemmons paid me a compliment that touched me deeply. He said that when we get to heaven he wants me to continue to be his partner. He's a Methodist, and I'm a Baptist, but I am convinced he will be there. And I, too, hope we can continue to work together.

Work in heaven? Yes, indeed! If there isn't any work there, it won't be heaven to Kemmons and me.

18

MISCELLANEOUS
REMINISCENCES

I think of a number of things I haven't mentioned yet but which might possibly be of interest. So this will be a miscellaneous catchall chapter. That will give me opportunity to flit around from subject to subject, as I often do when I'm just passing the time of day with friends.

I'll start with some surprises I have had in buying property for development. I've had some pretty amazing ones, all right, and I'll give you two examples—one happy, the other painful.

In 1964 my wife and I were instrumental in having Rosewood General Hospital built in Houston, Texas. It is a 180-bed hospital, erected and operated by a Texas non-profit organization under the auspices of the Wallace E. Johnson–E. B. McCool Foundation.

Later I asked my Houston representatives to negotiate

for the purchase of a tract of sixteen acres adjacent to the hospital. I saw the need for the construction of professional-type offices in the immediate area.

My agents reported that the tract could be bought for about $1,200,000. But there was a house on the far side of the tract, and the woman living there wouldn't sell unless we'd put a clause in the contract giving her the right to live there till she died. Well, I saw no serious objection to that. We wouldn't need that part of the tract for a long time. Besides, it didn't surprise me to learn there was a house on the acreage. When I buy tracts, I frequently find houses on them.

So I told my agents to proceed. It was O.K.

The contract was signed, and Wallace E. Johnson Enterprises proceeded to build a group of early-American-style office buildings close to the hospital property. As I say, there was a real need for them, and we quickly rented them when the project was completed. Since we couldn't fill the demand for space, we started construction of another complex to cost about $500,000.

One day—and this was about four years after I had bought the sixteen-acre tract—I got a call from our representative in charge of the property. He said the lady in the house on the far side, Mrs. W. E. Sampson, had died.

"What do you want done with the house?" he asked.

"Oh, I don't know," I said. "Board it up. I haven't any use for it. Forget it."

"You don't want to board up this house!" he said, and his tone indicated he thought I was crazy. "This is no ordinary house."

I had never seen the house and hadn't had any curiosity about it. I was interested only in the land—that part of the tract for future use.

"What's unusual about that house?" I asked.

And he told me—much to my astonishment. Why, it was a mansion! It was a reproduction of Mount Vernon, the home of George Washington.

Alma and I went to Houston to see it, and it made my eyes bulge. It was indeed a beautiful reproduction of Mount Vernon. And I had been carrying that "old house" at a valuation of one dollar on our books!

It needed some repairs and refurbishing and we put our professional decorators to work on it. We are keeping it as our Houston home—we go there occasionally—and it is quite a show place. It couldn't be reproduced today for less than $250,000.

But our No. 1 home and permanent base remains in Memphis.

Now I'll give you a vice-versa experience. I once lost a house without knowing it—till it was too late.

I made a down payment and signed a contract to purchase 225 acres near Memphis. There were several houses on the tract, and it was stipulated in the contract that if I tore down any houses, or if any were destroyed by fire, during the life of the mortgage, I would have to pay for them.

A year or so later the mortgagor called me up and said I owed him five thousand dollars more.

"What do you mean?" I asked. "Why do I owe you five thousand dollars more?"

"You had a house moved off the place," he said. "It was worth at least five thousand dollars."

I couldn't believe him. That was preposterous. I said I would investigate.

He was right. The man I had given permission to live in the house, in return for his keeping an eye on the whole property, had stolen the house. He had moved it piece by piece off my tract, and I was stuck for five thousand dollars.

Building materials and other things have been stolen from me, but that was the first time a whole house had been stolen. I am happy to report that such a theft hasn't been repeated.

Well, so much for surprises.

Right here might be a good place for me to tell you about the National Association of Home Builders and to pay tribute to that great organization for what it has meant to me and to others in the construction business. I am proud of my connection with it and the part I have played in its growth.

I fear that if it hadn't been for the National Association we would not today have free enterprise in our field. It might be completely controlled by the government.

Back during World War II, Ben Delugach, another home-builder, told me about a house organ published by the National Association of Home Builders, which then was a small organization as compared to its size today. Ben said their publication was very useful. It cost only ten dollars a year and kept you informed of all the latest news and developments of special interest to builders. It also kept you up to date on the government's rules and regulations governing priorities on materials, permits to build and all that sort of complicated thing.

I got interested in the National Association of Home Builders. It seemed to me that Memphis ought to have a local chapter. I invited seventeen builders to a luncheon at the Hotel Peabody to discuss the matter. Frank W. Cortright, the executive vice-president of the National, came down from Philadelphia and talked to us. He outlined the purposes and policies of the organization and sold us on it.

So we organized at that meeting, and the local builders

put the finger on me to be president. John B. Goodwin was elected vice-president and R. A. McDougal was elected secretary.

Shortly thereafter, Bob Gerholz, the national president, came to Memphis and really turned us on. He was from Flint, Michigan, and was a great speaker. He fired us up.

Well, as I have pointed out, that was during the war, and we builders were having difficulty in trying to get materials and workmen for private-enterprise construction. And then came a bombshell that threatened to blast us out of business.

President Franklin Roosevelt issued a decree that all private home-building be stopped—right now. That created a tremendous crisis for us. Most of us had projects under way. If we could not complete them and pay off, we'd be ruined.

The National Association called for an emergency conference in Washington. All of its officers were there, along with the Association's lawyer, Herb Colton. Local chapters around the country also were represented. I hurried to Washington, nearly scared to death. I had a lot of houses in various stages of construction.

A representative of the government spoke to us, and he was hard, tough and dictatorial. I asked him if he meant we couldn't even complete the jobs we had already started, and he said yes, he meant exactly that. We could not drive another blankety-blank nail. The order meant stop.

We made a strong plea for relaxation of the order, pointing out that we hadn't been given any warning or time limit. If enforced it would mean bankruptcy.

I came home greatly worried and soon had reason to be even more disturbed. Two of the top executives of the mortgage company with whom we were doing a large volume of business came to our offices to inform us that we would have to stop construction. They could not finance us another day. We were through.

I was already scared and jittery over the situation in the home-building business, and that announcement staggered me. I just sat there trembling, not knowing what to say.

But my wife, bless her heart, can usually think of something in an emergency. So she said to those two executives, "We owe you thousands of dollars. You want your money, don't you?"

They said, "Why, yes, indeed!"

"Then the only way in this world you can get it," Alma replied, "is to let us complete the houses we have half finished."

They left, with their order standing. But the next day they came back. They said their company had had a meeting, and they had decided to let us complete the unfinished houses. But when that was done, we were through.

"And I have some news for you," Alma replied. "When we finish these houses, you are right about our being through. We are through with you. We'll never ask you for another loan."

We finished those thirty houses. And due to the pleas and pressure from the National Association of Home Builders, the government relaxed its stop-work order. We stayed in business.

At that time the National Association was small. Its work in the crisis proved to builders all over the country that there was need for such an organization, and it has been growing in numbers and in prestige ever since. Today there are about 44,000 members, and it is doing a great job in helping the government to formulate and maintain a good, sound policy in regard to laws and regulations governing the home-building industry and in working for fair and harmonious relations between the builders, labor and the mortgage bankers.

Yes, I am proud that I had a part in that important meeting in Washington when the stop-work order was under fire. It was an historic occasion. I fear that if we had not met the issue head on without delay, the government would have taken over all home-building, and that would have ended private enterprise for us. Once the government takes over anything, it is awfully hard to get it to turn loose.

For a long time we stuck to our determination not to do any more business with that mortgage company, but they showed such a conciliatory spirit that in time we became friends again.

I don't see eye to eye with my fellow builders about everything. A lot of them make a great to-do over model homes. They build a show house, advertise it, whoop it up. They draw a lot of people to see it. Maybe that sort of stunt pays off for them, but it didn't pay off for me. I tried it once in cooperation with a big national magazine. We built a pretty house, furnished it artistically, and spent a lot of money advertising our opening. And people really responded. We must have drawn thirty thousand people one beautiful Sunday afternoon. There was a big traffic jam. Cars were stacked up for half a mile. I felt proud of our organization.

I like to know what people really think, not just what they tell me when they know who I am. So I turned up my collar, pulled down my hat and pretended to be just a passerby. I asked a man sitting impatiently at the wheel of a car caught in the jam what in the world was going on.

"Aw," he said, "it's that crazy Wallace Johnson. He's showing some kind of new house."

I got the picture. He was under pressure from his wife. He hadn't wanted to come to see the house in the first place, and after he got caught in that jam he was ready to fight. A beautiful day was ruined.

Now, I ask you—what chance did I have to sell that

fellow the model home? He felt like shooting Wallace Johnson.

Thousands of people saw our model home, but no one offered to buy it! Very few even asked the price. It was like people going to the circus. They like to see elephants, but nobody wants to buy one.

So I haven't built any more model homes in the generally accepted definition of that term. I have tried to build homes that ordinary people can afford and which they go to see with the thought of possibly buying—nice, comfortable homes to live in, not showrooms.

In running Wallace E. Johnson Enterprises and my other corporations, and in helping to operate the vast Holiday Inns organization, I am surrounded by brilliant associates, many of them young men. I respect their advice and am frequently guided by it—when I don't have a firm opinion of my own. But when I'm sure I'm right, I go ahead, sometimes much to their horror.

The Holmes Road subdivision is an example. When I bought that tract and discussed with my staff plans for developing it, they cautioned me to go slow. As they studied the maps, they pointed out that I was bottled up. I did not have an access road to the property. How could we build and sell homes to people when they couldn't get to them?

I listened to their vigorous protests, but I ordered the work to proceed. Go ahead. Build streets and houses. Yes, it was true that the surrounding property owners had refused to sell. We didn't have an access strip, but I had obtained permission from one owner for trucks to cross his property in getting to our tract with materials.

"We'll solve the access problem permanently when we have to," I said.

They thought I was a stubborn guy who was heading for a hard fall, but I had faith that if I built houses in that subdivision attractive enough and offered them for sale at a price low enough, I could sell them. And I knew that when I got people living in those houses, they'd help me get a permanent access road to them.

I ran ads in the paper admitting that the houses were hard to find, but they were such bargains that they were worth the effort. In fact, they were so hard to find that we couldn't give complete instructions in the ads. It was too confusing. So we just gave instructions on how to get so far and suggested that they then ask somebody for further directions.

We sold thirty houses the first two days the subdivision was opened, and the whole project worked out as I thought it would. We were able to buy a strip for an access road, when the people who had bought our houses helped us put the pressure on.

In that project, and in other difficult situations, I always have had the attitude that it can be done. With that positive attitude, and with the help of God, it usually works out that way. Sometimes when my key men come to me with baffling problems, I give them assignments that strike them as impossible. I frighten them. They express doubt and look at me as if they are sure I have lost my mind.

"Oh, you can do it," I assure them. "You can do it. Go to it."

My confidence in my idea, and my confidence in their ability to execute it, apparently inspires them. They usually find a way to do the "impossible."

I shall be indebted forever to many of the men and women I have been associated with in starting, building and operating my businesses, both in the early days and in more recent years. I have already mentioned some of them in previous chapters—Mr. and Mrs. Paul Harris, who came into the Wallace E. Johnson Enterprises office when

Alma and I were having to do all the work and were almost at the point of exhaustion; S. E. Carter, a splendid estimator and our first carpenter foreman; A. E. Neal, who was our purchasing agent during those difficult war years; Hamilton Smythe, Jr., our vice-president in charge of mortgages and a top trouble-shooter.

And a man to whom I shall forever be grateful is my good friend Grady Harrison. Back in 1940, when I was struggling to get started as a home-builder, Grady was the vice-president of the Ark-Mo Lumber Company and was in charge of their wholesale and retail yards in Memphis. They were a big outfit. I was then building my $2,999 homes and had very little capital. Soon after I started Wallace E. Johnson Enterprises, Grady solicited some of my business. I gave him an order for seventeen dollars worth of windows.

That started our association. I gave him more orders for lumber—and asked for credit. He extended it. We did a lot of business in the months that followed, but I had to keep asking for more and more credit. I was tying up a lot of materials in houses I hoped to sell when they were finished. My indebtedness to the Ark-Mo Lumber Company ran up to $100,000. And then Grady was called to the home office in Little Rock. They were alarmed about that fellow Wallace E. Johnson and the $100,000 he owed the company. According to the credit-rating agencies Johnson was an unknown. They wondered if their Memphis vice-president realized what he was doing.

Grady went to bat for me. He said he had faith and confidence in me and was sure I would pay off. He thought it was a good account.

"I'm doing the best I can over there in Memphis," he told the headquarters brass. "And if you don't think what I am doing is O.K., you can send somebody else to take over."

They were smart enough not to press Grady, for he was important to their operation.

I, of course, did pay off the $100,000 and continued to do a lot of business with Grady for the next twenty years. I bought about $1,000,000 worth of lumber from them.

When Grady left them and organized his own lumber company, our friendship continued and we became associated in some profitable lumber deals.

The names of others who have been so kind and helpful to me in my business career come to mind. Goodness, how could I ever have gotten along without S. O. Nabors? He was one of the best and most versatile workmen I have ever known. He could do anything and do it well—do carpentry, set tile, lay brick, hang paper. Many was the time he saved the day in an emergency.

And I mustn't forget John Fox. He was president of Commercial and Industrial Bank. One day when I was in the bank, he said, in a kidding way, "Wallace, I'd like to come out and work for you." And I laughed and said come on, we'd be mighty glad to have him.

I forgot the pleasant little exchange, but one day John called me up. "I'm leaving the bank," he said. "I'll be out Monday to go to work for you."

He came, and we made him a vice-president of Wallace E. Johnson Enterprises, and he contributed greatly to our success in the next few years. He handled financial matters, and at one time he boasted that he signed more checks than anybody else in Memphis. We had a payroll of $100,000 a week, and he signed all the checks. We were doing a volume of business then of from $12,000,000 to $15,000,000 a year, so he had a lot of check signing to do. We didn't have a computer to help, either.

I know I often seem to hire people on impulse, but usually I am being guided by more than snap judgment. I pride myself on being able to size up a person pretty accurately in a hurry. Many of the men who now hold key executive positions in my organizations were hired in that manner when they were young. They have fully justified my fast appraisal of their potential.

Take, for instance, Jack Rice, my assistant at Holiday Inns. A few years ago Jack was working for the Shelby United Neighbors, which is the Memphis Community Fund. One day he and his boss called on me to ask for a donation. I talked with them a few minutes and was favorably impressed by Jack. He struck me as a bright young man with a good personality, one who had great possibilities.

"All right," I said to the top Community Fund man, "I'll give you a good donation on one condition—that you let your young friend here come to work for me."

They were both taken aback. Jack didn't know what to say. He, of course, had never given a moment's thought to the possibility of coming to work for Wallace E. Johnson at Holiday Inns.

But we made a deal. Jack quit the Community Fund job and came to work for me. I haven't ever regretted my impulsive and rather whimsical action that day.

Robert E. Hansom is president of Medical Development Services, Inc., a company which handles millions and millions of dollars a year. He worked himself up to that top spot in just a few years. And, frankly, I almost overlooked Bobby.

One morning when I arrived at my office I found him waiting for me. He was then a young man just out of school. I had my mind on lots of things and was in a rush. I asked him what he wanted, and he said a job.

"Sorry, son," I said. "We just don't have anything open for a young man like you right now. Maybe some other time."

And I hurried on into my office.

The next morning he was back in my outer office, waiting for me again. I looked at him with some irritation.

"What do you want now?" I asked.

"I still want a job," he said.

"I told you yesterday we didn't have anything," I replied. "That still stands."

The following morning—there was Bobby again. There seemed to be no getting rid of the boy.

"Just what kind of work do you think you can do?" I asked.

"I'm willing to do anything to get a start," he said.

"O.K.," I said. "Get a broom and start sweeping."

But we didn't actually make a janitor out of him. We gave him some kind of little clerical job as a sort of test. By that time I was impressed by his persistence, his determination and his good humor. I began to see the young man for what he was. His rise in our organization was steady.

I met Roland Maddox, who became president of Wallace E. Johnson Enterprises, under more leisurely circumstances, and I saw his potential at once. He had just finished at the University of Mississippi and had come to Memphis looking for a job. Roland was ambitious for a business career. He came to see me, and I invited him to have lunch. I knew that would give me a chance to ask him some questions and to size him up.

He was a smart, good-looking young man, and it didn't take me thirty minutes to see he would produce if given the chance. I hired him as we ate our dessert.

I hired Erie Henrich even quicker. He has been my tax attorney for many years. Before we moved to our present address, our backyard adjoined Erie's backyard. One afternoon we spoke to each other over the fence. I asked how he was, and he said he was a little excited. He had just resigned as an attorney for the Internal Revenue Service and was starting out on his own.

"Then I'd like to be your first client," I said.

I didn't know a lot about his ability, but he was a good neighbor and citizen. And certainly he had the right tax background to do a good job in private practice. We have hit it off just fine.

In hiring young men I have a little test I give them without their realizing what I am doing. I size them up as we shake hands and exchange pleasantries. And then I say, "All right, let's get down to business." I ask six or eight questions in rapid-fire order, without giving him a chance to answer. I say:

"Tell me about yourself, young man. What do you want in life? Are you a money-maker or a money-spender? Do you think you can take authority and be promoted and still keep your feet on the ground? Can you get along with people? What grades did you make in school? What are your working habits? How much money do you want?"

And then I stop and see how he reacts. If he can remember all those questions without asking me to repeat any of them, and if he gives me good, sound, honest answers, I am favorably impressed and feel that I am not taking too great a risk in hiring him. I hire him on the spot. He can answer all questions of the personnel department later. I already know what I want to know.

Once in a great while I am disappointed in a young man I hire in my fast, impulsive way, but not often. I think my system will stand comparison with other and more exhaustive systems.

Many people may have the impression that there are no more pleasant, clean-cut, ambitious young people left who believe in the American system, that they are all shaggy-haired, unkempt, cynical young rebels and revolutionaries who are against everything that has made this country great and which most of us older people hold dear and sacred. But that isn't true. The young militants and rebels are in the minority. We don't have any trouble finding the kinds of young people we want in our organizations, and I know many other employers can say that, too.

What's ahead in the home building industry? A great boom, because there is no getting around the fact that there is a tremendous housing shortage in America. We need millions of new homes to relieve overcrowding in the ghettos and in the poverty sections of cities and to replace homes of substandard construction. And I think that within the next decade we are going to get them. But we can't get them through regular construction methods. They are too slow, and there are not enough construction workers to build them. Under our present methods we can't even hold our own, to say nothing of making headway, for the population increases faster than we can build houses.

But I predict that we will lick the problem through the industrialized home. The industrialized home goes a step beyond the prefabricated home. It doesn't come with all the parts cut, ready to be fitted together. It comes already made in whole units produced in factories, ready to be placed on a foundation. A crane, for instance, will lift a finished bathroom off a truck and set it down. Hook it up to the water line, and you are ready to take a bath. And it will be the same way with the kitchen and other rooms. You will be able to set up a complete home in a few hours.

Homes in the future will be produced on production lines just as automobiles are produced today. It's coming.

19

THE OTHER PHONE CALL

Now let me tell you about a memo I wrote that turned out to be a boomerang.

In the first chapter I mentioned the important part telephone calls played in my life, and I said that two of those calls stood out in my mind as the most important of all. I gave an account of the circumstances surrounding the first call—the one that came from Kemmons Wilson one night in 1953, when he asked me to join him in founding Holiday Inns.

In the chapters that followed, I told you how that call led to the development of the world's largest hotel-motel organization.

Now the time has come to tell you about the other "most important call." It came twenty-four years after the first call. The two calls are related, for if it had not been for the first, the second would not have come. It very probably will mark the beginning of my epilogue, the climax, of my life. As I look back now, I am convinced that all that went before was just God's way of preparing me for the great task I now have undertaken.

Here is the background that led to this call:

On the fifteenth of September, 1976, I went into Kemmons's office and told him that on October 5, 1976, I would be seventy-five years old and felt that I should retire. He said, "Partner, I do not want to lose you." But he knew my mind was made up. Toward the end of our talk, Kemmons said, "Partner, your birthday comes up at the beginning of the International Holiday Inn conference. I would like the privilege of announcing your decision when the franchise holders from all over the world are attending the conference."

At about 11:30 A.M. on October 6, Kemmons went to the podium and made the following remarks: "This is an extremely sad moment in my life. My partner, Wallace Johnson, has advised me that he wants to retire as of January 1, 1977. I told him at that moment that I did not want to lose him, that we had been so close for so many years." Unbeknownst to me, he had invited Bob Gerholz from Flint, Michigan, and Clem Stone from Chicago, along with other friends of mine, to be present at the conference.

Kemmons had many kind words to say about our working together for this long period of time; but the words that have been ringing in my ears ever since were these: "I know not which one of us will get to heaven first, but just in case Wallace gets there before I do, when I get there I will knock on Saint Peter's door and say, 'Where is Wallace?' He will say, 'He's working right around the corner.' And then I will say to Saint Peter, 'I want you to give me Wallace as my partner for eternity in Heaven.'"

You can well believe that was very touching and very emotional; and by that time there were few dry eyes among the more than two thousand attending that meeting.

In addition to what Kemmons had to say, Clem Stone presented to me a special award from Religious Heritage of America, which was very touching; and Bob Gerholz also brought an award that I will remember all the days of my life. I went to the podium and very emotionally thanked Kemmons to the best of my ability. I said that it was also my desire that the two of us spend eternity in Heaven. "Of all the years that Kemmons and Wallace have been partners on projects from a hundred dollars on up to millions," I told the audience, "we've never had a lawyer to write a contract between the two of us. We were able to have faith and confidence in each other and our word to each other was all we needed."

At that time I was asked to continue to serve on the board of directors and on the executive committee. Kemmons also asked that I serve as consultant to Holiday Inns. I continue to receive reports and keep up with activities daily and weekly.

I had no way of knowing that out in California and Texas events were shaping up that would soon have me involved in a new, worldwide undertaking.

One day I had two visitors from out of town—Dr. Bill Bright and Dr. Joe L. Mayes. Dr. Bright is president of Campus Crusade for Christ, with headquarters in San Bernardino, California. Dr. Mayes, president of Mayes International in Dallas, Texas, is an enthusiastic supporter of Campus Crusade.

Why did they come to see me? Well, they wanted to tell me about Campus Crusade for Christ, and try to get me interested. I knew a little about the organization, had read about the good work they had done through the years, but had to confess that I did not know very much. They briefed me on its history and work.

I learned that Campus Crusade for Christ was started

by Bill Bright and his wife, Vonette, in a very small way on the campus of the University of California twenty-five years ago—just the two of them talking to students about the better, happier, more successful life to be found through Christ here on earth and salvation in Heaven through eternity.

From that humble beginning, Campus Crusade has spread around the world. As they talked, I recalled reading in the newspapers about their tremendous Here's Life, America campaigns all over the country, and I remembered the tremendous "Explo '72" in Dallas, when over eighty thousand crusade workers converged on Dallas to study, pray, witness, and dedicate their lives to Christian service. The week was climaxed with a rally of one hundred fifty-thousand, the largest gathering of its kind in history.

But Bill and Joe said that, as large as "Explo '72" was, it was eclipsed by "Explo '74" in Seoul, South Korea, which drew 1.5 million for a week of intensive training.

They gave me more facts and figures and explained that, although Campus Crusade was started on a campus and for a while was concerned mostly with college students, it had long since broadened its territory to include younger people, older people, professional people, poor people, rich people—everybody. And, although it was nondenominational, it worked with churches. In fact, it depended upon church groups to a large extent.

I soon caught Bill's and Joe's fervor about Campus Crusade. And then they came to the point of their visit. Although the crusade had done—and was still doing—a tremendous job, they felt it could, and should, do an even bigger one. They told me about a new campaign in the planning stage, greater than anything the organization had ever done before, greater than the "Explos." The new crusade would be known as Here's Life. It would take the good news of Jesus Christ and the Gospel to every nation on earth! It would fulfill the great commission in this generation!

They shared the vision that such a program, based on Old and New Testament prophecy, could change the world from one of violence, crime, immorality, racial unrest and bitterness, jealousy and materialism to the world of peace, beauty, and brotherhood that God intended it to be.

We in Religious Heritage of America, an organization of which I am the national honorary chairman, also had been saying that Christ was the only hope of saving a world hell-bent on its own destruction, so I agreed with Bill and Joe. OK, but what did they want me to do?

Well, they said they were forming a committee to find the right man to serve as international chairman of the new crusade, a program that would require the raising of millions of dollars if it were to be done in the big way they envisioned. Would I serve as a member of the committee to find an international chairman? I said I would be glad to serve.

Then they made another request. Would I write a memo outlining the qualifications I thought the international chairman should have? I agreed to do that.

I gave the matter some thought during the next few days, prayed over it, and then wrote Dr. Joe Mayes that I thought the man selected should have these qualifications:

1. This man should be a born-again Christian and ready to say to the world that Jesus Christ is the answer to the world's problems.

2. This man needs to be a great leader in the United States and, since this is a worldwide program, he should be a man whose name is tied to a company that is internationally known and carries weight around the world, which is something this program will need.

3. This man should have the respect and admiration of the industry he serves.

4. He should be a man capable of speaking to large groups of men and women and effective in getting his points across—telling of the opportunities we have to sell the world on Christ.

5. He should be able to spend time traveling around the world with Dr. Bill Bright and others to tell the story.

I am sure that if each of us will spend time in prayer that God will reveal to us the right man for this great undertaking.

Several weeks passed, and I did not hear any more about the search for a man to be international chairman. And, to tell you the truth, the matter passed out of mind as I kept busy with other things.

Then came the important phone call I mentioned at the beginning of this chapter. The call came from Bill Bright. It was time for the committee to meet and consider the selection of a chairman for Here's Life, and he thought Memphis would be a good place for the meeting.

I said, "Sure! I'll serve you breakfast."

So Bill Bright, Joe Mayes, and Bunker Hunt came. Roy Rogers and Dale Evans were very much interested, but commitments prevented their coming. They sent Art Rush, their business manager, to assure us they were with us. Jim McKinney and Doug Dillard, representing Campus Crusade, also came with them.

Bill talked to us about the work and the scope of the new campaign. And then he said to me: "Wallace, we have had a committee meeting, and have decided on the man we want to head the international campaign. . . ."

I was taken aback and a bit miffed. They had had a meeting of the committee and had decided on the man? Why, I was a member of the committee, yet they had had the meeting without me. But I tried not to show I was hurt by the slight. I said, "You mean to tell me you've already made the selection?"

He said, "Yes," and then pointed his finger at me: "And that man is *you.*"

That staggered me. I was sort of tongue-tied, but I did manage to stammer out a protest. Oh, no! No, I was not the man for the job. In listing the qualifications I thought the man should have, it certainly had never occurred to me that I had them.

"Why," I said, "I can't read, I can't talk, I can't write, I'm seventy-five years old—too old."

But they insisted I was the man. I thought of Moses and the three years he went around wishing he could find a doctor when he tried to avoid the Lord's work. So I agreed to give it a lot of prayerful thought and would let them have my answer later.

Alma and I went home that night and prayed for God's guidance in making a decision.

The next day I asked the advice of my long-time business partner and friend, Kemmons Wilson. I said, "Will you please tell me why I should say no to this call from Campus Crusade?"

He said, "Wallace, you can't say no."

I always have had great respect for his judgment, but I couldn't agree with him that time. It seemed unwise—perhaps a bit absurd—for me to take on such a heavy assignment at my stage in life. Why, they were talking about a campaign that would require millions of dollars! To take the Gospel to every nation on earth would require every known means of communication and thousands of dedicated workers.

Although the enormity of the project frightened me, I

could not evade the challenge of it. My conscience kept pricking me when I tried to use age as an excuse to say no. I read my Bible and learned that Moses was eighty-five when God called him to be the leader of the Israelites. He said he couldn't talk, and God said he would provide someone for that.

After about four weeks of praying, arguing with myself, and asking the advice of friends, I told Alma on Sunday morning that I could no longer carry the burden of indecision. It was tearing me to pieces. I wrote Bill Bright a letter. That was on April 22, 1977. I said:

April 22, 1977

Dr. Bill Bright, President
Campus Crusade for Christ International
Arrowhead Springs
San Bernardino, California 92414

Dear Dr. Bright:

Alma and I have spent many hours in prayer, searching for God's will in our lives, to answer the request that we assist in a worldwide program, with you and many others, in the campaign to raise funds to continue to tell the world about the love that our Savior Jesus Christ has for each one of us.

I do not know of a decision that Alma and I have spent more time on than this request. I talked with my partner, Kemmons Wilson, hoping that he might give me some good reason that I could use to say no to your request, and I tried to the best of my ability to say no as Moses tried to say no to God thousands of years ago.

My partner, Kemmons said, "Wallace, you can't say no," and at this moment I have not found an honest way to say no. Therefore, I must submit and say that if this is what God would have me to do to assist you and the others to tell the story to the world about our Lord and Savior Jesus Christ and that He loves all of us, I am ready to start to work.

Dr. Bright, there are many details and questions that I have in my mind, but I do not think this is the proper time to go into detail, but only trust in God that he will grant us the wisdom from day to day.

We thank God for you and Vonette and for the great work that you are doing around the world, and pray that He will continue to give all of us the wisdom to do His will. May God continue to give you the strength, wisdom and power throughout the years to come.

Sincerely yours,

Wallace E. Johnson

So, I accepted the call and since then have been out of my short retirement, almost as busy as I was during the years I put in fourteen- and sixteen-hour days for Holiday Inns, Johnson Enterprises, and forty other corporations. And although I shall not make a dime in material gain this time around, I already am receiving spiritual dividends that are enriching my life. I have had the opportunity to discuss it with friends around the world. They are saying, "Wallace, the program has definitely got to be carried on. The world has tried everything else, and now it must try

Christ. If we don't get at it without further delay, it will be too late."

W. Clement Stone, the Chicago insurance man and philanthropist, is an old, dear friend of mine. I have talked with him about this and he, among others, has urged me on, has given me courage. Clem Stone has agreed to serve on the executive committee with me. I am still a little frightened when I think that never in the history of mankind has there been a program such as we are undertaking, but I have faith that God will provide the wisdom we need. And, as I have said, I believe that all of my previous life has been a preparation for this.

With all the work involved in such an effort, I knew I would need an assistant. That bright, energetic, dedicated young man is John Butler. He is experienced in management as well as in public relations and advertising and is enthusiastic about the crusade.

In 1977, John Butler was selected as one of the Outstanding Young Men in America and has quite a background for a young man twenty-seven years old. He has served as assistant to a college president, assistant to Dr. Mayes at Mayes International, and as president of his own company. He worked his way through high school and college in radio and television and graduated with honors from the University of Texas in Austin.

John's beautiful wife, Beverly, has also been a source of inspiration to Alma and me. She has a great voice and I love to hear her sing. When she sings "The Lord's Prayer" acapella I am deeply moved.

I am depending upon John to carry much of the load of activities at the office in Memphis as well as to make trips on my behalf. The first month John joined me, we traveled twenty thousand miles together in the interests of the program.

We will work in and out of the international offices in Memphis. But, of course, much of the program and all of the regular work of Campus Crusade for Christ will continue to be handled at Crusade headquarters, Arrowhead Springs, San Bernardino, California 92414.

Roy Rogers, movie and television star, is the international vice-chairman, and Texas oil man, Bunker Hunt, is the chairman of the executive committee. I don't think we could find two better qualified men to lean upon.

An International Sponsoring Committee to support this great effort has been formed. It is a group of some of the world's most outstanding leaders. Included are concerned Christian men and women from business, government, the professions, sports, education, labor, entertainment, the arts, and, of course, religion. Approximately one thousand world leaders will serve on this committee.

Now, how are we going to raise the large sums of money necessary to carry the Gospel around the world in the next few years? Well, first of all we are depending upon God to provide the means, for we believe this crusade is within His will. But we also know that God works through human beings His wonders to perform, so we are praying that thousands of people of all nationalities, rich, poor, and middle class, will see the vision of a better world and will support us with their prayers and contributions. We must also go after large gifts. We are seeking people who believe in our goal. We pray that the example of the original widow's mite, which was blessed by Jesus, will inspire affluent people to proportionate giving to enable the over four billion people in the world to learn of the good news of Christianity.

Yes, it will take sacrifices of time, talent, and money by many to reach the goal of sharing with the world what I feel is the only *real* hope for us all.

This goal should be the personal goal of every Christian. To do the job, each individual, every group must play a part. Campus Crusade's Here's Life will be working hand in hand with all Christian denominations and organizations as God leads. We also will be working with agnostics and atheists, people who want a better world in the sweet now-and-now, even if they are uncertain about one in the sweet by-and-by. There is purpose enough in this for people of all persuasions.

One such organization is Religious Heritage of America, which already is playing a vital part in God's master plan. This is one of the finest groups of dedicated men and women that I have ever had the privilege of working with.

The Rediscover America Program, one effort of Religious Heritage of America, is focused on Judeo-Christian principles that have made America great. Its purpose is to help communities rediscover honesty and integrity and the other Christian principles that are so basic to our democratic way of life. In turn, this should lead to the reduction of crime. It is so important that each of us support these programs, otherwise we may not have an America to sell America to.

It is my hope and prayer that you will be inspired to become actively involved in your local church, along with other organizations that are working to share Christ with the world.

20

OUR GREATEST
THREAT

A man asked me the other day what I thought was the greatest threat to the United States and our way of life.

Was it worldwide communism? The race problem? Inflation and the economic situation? Was it immorality, corruption, atheism, crime, cynicism? Was it bureaucracy?

I said all those things are grave problems, all right, but the single greatest threat to our democracy, our way of life, is that of having the wrong attitude.

He asked me what I meant by "the wrong attitude." I said the wrong attitude toward everything. Too many of our people have the wrong attitude toward God, the wrong attitude toward our country and our flag, the wrong attitude toward their families and their jobs, the wrong attitude toward society, the wrong attitude toward people who don't agree with them about everything, the wrong attitude toward morality and honesty. Just go on and name it, and you find that too many people have the wrong attitude toward it. They have a negative, cynical, grasping, sick attitude toward everything when they should have a positive, constructive, determined, happy attitude toward life and our problems and opportunities.

We have hundreds of employees in our organizations, and it is both inspiring and depressing to see how they react to situations.

X is a bright, eager, hardworking, ambitious man. He does a good job, and we think highly of him. We feel he has a good future with us.

Y, too, is a good man and has a position equal in rank to X's. Also like X, he is ambitious and has a lot on the ball. We have him in mind, too, for more responsibility in the future.

A better position above both of them opens up, and we decide that still another employee, Z, is better qualified at the time to step into it.

Now what happens? X feels that he hasn't been treated fairly. He should have that promotion. He becomes disgruntled, sour, irritable. His whole personality changes. His associates avoid him. His work suffers. We try to be patient with him, feeling that with a little time he will snap out of it and become himself again. We assure him that he has a good future with us. Just go ahead and do a good job, we say, and your turn will come.

But X can't, or won't, change his attitude toward us, his job, his associates. He is sore at the whole world. He makes serious mistakes in his work. He is a discredit to our organization. Our patience runs out, and we reluctantly and sadly have to let him go.

But what about Y who also didn't get the promotion he felt he deserved? Naturally, he is disappointed, too, but he doesn't let it sour him. He seems even more determined to do a better job, to improve in knowledge and ability. He is still pleasant to work with. He shows us he is ready for something better whenever we say the word. And sooner or later, we say it. We'd be crazy not to.

Now, why is X a failure and Y a success? Both have equal ability. It is simply a matter of attitude.

Much of what I see and hear and read about in every field of life today distresses me. It shocks me when I read that some professor has told his students that God is dead, that Christ is merely a legendary figure, and that religion is a fraud. I certainly consider that a wrong and shocking attitude.

And the idea that anything you can get by with is permissible is also the wrong attitude. The idea that the world owes you a living and you are going to see that you get it even if you have to kill and steal is wrong. The idea that your job is just drudgery, something you are forced to do, is the wrong attitude. The idea that you are not your brother's or your family's keeper and that you have no obligation to try to make the world a little better is the wrong attitude.

The number of people in this country with the wrong attitude has reached dangerous proportions, and it seems to be increasing. We must reverse the trend somehow. If we can, then our other big problems will be much easier to solve, for, indeed, they are the symptoms of our illness, not the illness itself. The illness is wrong "attituditis."

It isn't easy to maintain a positive, cheerful, consistently right attitude. We all have periods of negativism, irritation, and discouragement, but if basically we have the right attitude, we can overcome them.

A friend once told me he had heard that I talk to myself and wanted to know if it was true.

"Why, certainly it is true," I said. "I talk to myself in the mirror every morning when I'm shaving. I think every man should look himself in the eye now and then and give

himself a good lecture. Helps to keep him in the right attitude toward life and himself."

"Well," my friend said, "you are a big shot, and you can
talk to yourself without anybody's thinking you are a nut.
But if I were to do that, folks would say I was off my
rocker. Might even have me committed."

Maybe some people say that about me, but if they do, it
doesn't bother me. I find it helpful to be honest and out-
spoken with myself—to express my self-criticism vocally.
And as I told my friend, I find that the older I get, the
harder it is to keep the old man in line. I need more dress-
ings-down then ever. When I finish shaving, I look at myself and may say something like this:

"Wallace, you didn't do so well yesterday. You didn't
have the right attitude at that conference. You were a
stumbling block, not a help. You want to watch that. You
must do better today."

Or I say something like this:

"Wallace, you acted like a stuffed shirt yesterday. You
gave that fellow who came to see you a rather brusque
brush-off. That wasn't the right attitude, and you know it.
You must be kinder and more patient, no matter how big a
hurry you are in. You've got to be a better Christian."

To talk to myself after shaving is just as much a part of
my routine as it is to put lather on my face. It is my way
of starting the day.

That's not the only time I talk to myself. All during the
day, when I realize I have acted unwisely or badly, I
pause for a moment and give myself an audible lecture. I
have a large oil portrait of myself, and I occasionally stand
and gaze at it for a few moments, but I do so in a spirit
of humility, not vanity. At such times I am pretty critical
of that fellow facing me, and I get him told.

In lecturing myself for my shortcomings, however, I
always end on a positive note. I tell myself that I must and

can do better. I tell myself, as Christ told the woman caught in adultery, to go and sin no more. Being human, I know that I will continue to make mistakes, but the big sin is in not trying to do better.

If God can forgive us for our sins and errors—and He can and does when we ask Him to—then surely we can forgive ourselves. But many people don't forgive themselves. Many make mistakes, and it ruins their whole lives from then on. They dwell on their sins and thus doom themselves to a life of failure and misery. They have a wrong attitude, a negative attitude.

I don't think there is a soul in this world who hasn't done some things for which he is ashamed—things that he'd never want to repeat. Sometimes in speeches I say I have invented one of the most marvelous machines anyone could dream of. You hook it up and turn it on, and it projects a picture on the wall. It shows your whole life from your babyhood—everything bad, dishonest, mean, contemptible, as well as everything good, kind, charitable, noble. You see yourself all along the way of life, all the wrong decisions you've made. It is indeed an amazing machine I have invented, and the price is reasonable. And then I ask my audience if anybody wants to buy it. If so, hold up your hand.

Nobody, of course, wants such a machine. If I really had one, I couldn't sell it. Who would like to see his whole life revealed in all its details? It would be too embarrassing, too painful. No, it is best that we not relive our mistakes, that we forgive ourselves and look forward, not backward.

I ask God to forgive me for my sins and mistakes of various kinds, and I know He does. Then I forgive myself. I am ready for a fresh start right then and there. I don't have to wait for the beginning of a new year.

This matter of attitude is important to every facet of

our civilization. Perhaps one of the answers to the ghetto problems in our cities—and perhaps the best answer—lies in changing the attitude of the people who live in them. Their attitude of defeatism, despair, and cynicism must change to an attitude of hope. We must provide them with training for useful and interesting jobs, inspire ambition in them, and show them that if they are willing to cooperate and work, they can raise their standard of life.

We must give poor people an incentive to work, not an incentive to remain idle. That is the road to better things for them and for society. I am speaking, of course, of people on relief who are physically able to work. Those who aren't must be taken care of through proper agencies.

Some cynical people say what's the use of trying to prepare for better jobs when computers will soon make them unnecessary? I do not share such a negative opinion. A computer has never caused us to release a man in our business. Computers can give a lot of information in a hurry, but it is information that human beings previously put into them. The machines can be of great assistance, but men and women have to make, service and operate the machines. And there will always be other kinds of work for people to do under our free-enterprise system—for those with the right attitude.

21

IF I HAD MY LIFE
TO LIVE OVER

Some people fear old age, but I don't. As I look into the future, I am full of happy expectation and excitement. I feel as Robert Browning did when he wrote: "Grow old along with me; the best is yet to be."

I believe that. And Jesus said that all things are possible to him who believes.

There are thousands of miracles waiting to be performed, and I want to help perform some of them. At least I shall have fun trying.

When I was born in 1901, scholars were predicting that the sum of human knowledge would double during the twentieth century. And we know it didn't take half that long. Now I read that the sum of knowledge will keep doubling at an amazing rate in the decades ahead.

Think what that means. It means marvelous new worlds are going to be discovered and developed. Amazing new inventions in every field are going to change our civilization. Life at the end of this century will be as different from life today as life now is different from the horse-and-buggy days when I was born.

As I look back over my life, and as I survey my situation in the present, I have a feeling of satisfaction and gratitude for what I have been able to accomplish with the help of God, a good wife and lots of friends. Ingratitude is a rather common fault, especially in this day and time, and I strive not to be guilty of it. I am truly grateful for a busy, interesting life and many, many blessings.

When reporters interview older people, to get information for biographical articles about them, it seems to be a standard question to ask: "If you had your life to live over, would you make a lot of changes?"

When I am asked that, I say, "No, I think I'd let my life alone." But I don't say it boastfully. I say it gratefully.

Oh, I'd make some changes—profit by some mistakes. I certainly wouldn't try to get into the cattle business again, for instance. But, in the main, I'd want my life to be what it has been.

I'm sure I'd want the same parents. I don't think any boy ever had better or more understanding parents than I had. As I said in a previous chapter, they didn't have money, but they were rich in their love for God, their children and their fellow man, and rich in character, industry, integrity.

And if I were living my life over again, I'd certainly want to accept Jesus Christ as my Savior as a boy and strive to live up to His teachings, just as I have done.

I know I'd want the same girl to be my wife. Alma has been not only a perfect wife but a wise and inspiring business partner from the very beginning of our life together. I couldn't find a better one. She has come up with ideas in emergencies that have been our business salvation. We were in love when we married, and we are still in love. Every morning when I leave home, after we have fixed breakfast together and have thanked God for His blessings, she walks to the door with me. We kiss goodbye, and she says, "I'll be praying for you today." And her remark is no mere pleasantry. She means it, and I know she means it. That helps when the going gets difficult.

If I had my life to live over, again I'd still want to be a home builder. I would want to start as a boy carpenter and learn the business as a workman as well as a contractor and developer.

And, of course, I again would want to keep growing and expanding my operations into many fields. I would want to team up with Kemmons Wilson in building the world's largest hotel-motel chain and in organizing and operating real estate and construction corporations. If I looked the world over I couldn't find a better or more compatible partner. I am lucky to be associated with a man of his administrative ability, keen foresight, drive, integrity and good humor.

That also goes for my brother-in-law, Barney McCool, who has played such an important part in all our enterprises for many years. If I were starting over, I'd certainly want him with me all the way.

But here's something that may surprise you. If I had it all to do over again, I think I'd still be a school drop-out.

As you may recall, if you have read the first part of this book, I dropped out of high school and went to work as a carpenter. I loved to saw and hammer and nail, loved to build, and got so much pleasure out of that kind of work that I was sure I was doing what God meant for me to do. And so, feeling as I did, I just couldn't resist the temptation of high wages—$1.50 an hour was big money to a seven-teen-year-old boy—and I dropped out of school and went to work.

Several years later I became convinced that I had made a mistake by dropping out of school, and I went back at the age of twenty—and finished high school at twenty-two. It wasn't easy—I was embarrassed to be so big and so old in a class with boys and girls much younger—but I stuck it out.

Now, since I decided that dropping out of school was a mistake, I may seem a bit contradictory when I say I probably would do it all over again. Wouldn't I profit by the mistake and stick in school from the beginning to graduation?

Well, as I look at my life from this long perspective, I can see now that my dropping out of school when I did wasn't such a mistake after all. Not for me. I felt capable of doing a man's work and was eager to be grown up, a big shot. I was full of ambition and energy that had to have a vent. And I was a bit scornful of school. It was for kids.

But after being out of school several years, and after seeing my own limitations and some of the advantages enjoyed by high-school graduates, I got a better appreciation for schooling than I would have gotten, perhaps, if I had never dropped out. I went back with a seriousness and a determination that my younger schoolmates lacked.

So it all worked out well for me. I think I'd repeat the schedule.

But don't misunderstand me. I certainly am not recommending that any boy or girl drop out of high school. Whether to drop out or not depends on the individual and the circumstances, but on the whole, I would advise strongly against it.

Now, what about college? I didn't go to college, although at one time I was eager to go. After I finished high school, however, I felt that I couldn't afford it. It wasn't as easy then for a boy to finance his way through college as it is now. Today any boy, if he really wants to, can go to college. Perhaps if I had wanted to go badly enough I could have found a way. But I didn't.

I have never felt handicapped because I didn't go to college. Whether a college education, or degree, is necessary depends to a large extent on what you want to do in life. It is absolutely necessary if you want to work in some fields and get ahead—if you want to be a doctor or a teacher, for instance. And I think it is advisable, generally speaking, as a foundation for success in almost any field.

But I also am convinced that today we are sending boys and girls to four- and five-year colleges, to work for degrees, who shouldn't go there. Many of them should be going to vocational schools, to take two-year courses instead of four-year courses, or five- and six-year courses. Not everyone is suited by intellect, temperament, ability, talent and interest to work for a degree, but many of them are pressured by their families and friends into going to college because that is the accepted thing, because it will get them out of the blue-collar class into the white-collar class. And, of course, many others go to college because they think it will be lots of fun—football games, fraternity parties, demonstrations and other excitement. And that's not a valid reason for going.

Millions of our young people are better suited to be mechanics, electricians, carpenters, plumbers, brick masons, stenographers, cooks, technicians, than they are suited to be lawyers, doctors, scientists, teachers, business administrators, statesmen. They can get the foundation they need in high school and the training in two-year vocational schools.

Many go to four-year colleges without the proper qualifications and motives, without knowing what it is they want in life, and they flunk out, or barely squeeze through, and end as cynical, frustrated misfits.

So, as I look at my own life as objectively as I can, I think I can stick to my original statement. If I had my life to live over, I think I'd live it pretty much as I have.

My partner, Kemmons Wilson, didn't go to college either, and I think he feels about his life as I feel about mine.

But we are both strong for higher education. His children are all college graduates, and if Alma and I had any children, we'd certainly want them to go. But I don't think we'd pressure them into going if they didn't want to go.

And while we are looking backward, let me tell you something that gives Alma and me a lot of satisfaction. Often, as we drive across our city, we pass homes that we built and sold years ago, and we go through whole residential sections that we developed—tracts that once were farm lands outside the city. It gives us pleasure, for example, to see the way we have contributed to the growth of Memphis, and we get even more pleasure out of seeing happy children playing on the lawns of those homes. We recall many heart-warming experiences in selling couples—some old and some young—the first home they ever owned and seeing them glow with excitement and pride when they ful for them. It gave them a new feeling of self-respect, moved in. Owning their own home did something wonderful for them. It gave them a new feeling of self-respect, purchase of a home is the most important purchase a couple can make.

So, as we drive around, we recognize "our" homes, and they stir happy memories. Many of them are still occupied by the original purchasers. They speak to us, tell us how much they have enjoyed their homes and what it has meant to them in rearing their families.

We are still getting rich dividends of our efforts of years ago. Yes, we have had a good life.

And as Kemmons and I take inventory of Holiday Inns, Inc., we naturally feel pride in what we have accomplished in twenty-four short, busy years. There are now more than 1,700 Holiday Inns, and new ones open with regularity. Several new ones have been opened in Africa recently, and we see great opportunity there. We expect our whole Holiday Inn program to continue to grow.

If I had my life to live over, I'd certainly want to repeat my Holiday Inn experience, although at times it was a long, rocky road. But travel hardships make arrival comforts all the more enjoyable.

When I went into semiretirement early in 1977, I learned something. I like to be busy—not even half-speed for me. I am more relaxed when I am busy. So now, along with my work with Holiday Inns, my other business interests, Religious Heritage of America and the Rediscover America Program, and as chairman of Here's Life Program, I am still hard at work, eager and happy in accepting new great challenges.

I know, of course, that we all must die some day. When my time comes, I hope it will be while I am in the middle of another exciting excursion into a new field, or while trying to do something for the glory of God and the betterment of mankind. I can no longer conceive of myself as inactive, even though I might be confined to a wheelchair. I will adapt and be as active as God allows.

There are going to be just as many opportunities for growth in the future as there are now—or have been in the past. Everything manufactured and used in this country is being improved or completely changed from year to year—

homes, commercial buildings, airplanes, automobiles, factories, computerized methods of production, communication systems. Everything is changing. It is a thrilling
concept to anyone with imagination and ambition.

My wife shares with me this enthusiasm about the future, just as she has shared the dreams we have made come
true in the past. I don't know of any couple who have a
more exciting life than we have, although we don't drink,
gamble, go in for parties or so-called high society, big-game
hunting, yachting, or other activities that many people
associate with "living it up." We live it up, but in our way.
We get fun and excitement out of exploring—exploring
new ideas and opportunities, exploring new ways to help
people find a better life.

Some cynics may say, "Oh, sure! There are plenty of
opportunities for guys with money to invest, but what about
little fellows without any dough?"

I say there are opportunities in this country everywhere
for everybody. The little fellow can start out in a small
way, work hard, save some money, and grow. Goodness
knows, Kemmons Wilson and I started out in a small way.
In fact, we started with nothing. No boys have had more
humble beginnings. What we have done, others can do.

But it isn't a desire for more and more money that moti-
vates us. We keep interested and busy in business because
it is a way of life and a fascinating game for us. We get a
kick out of creating a new project and more jobs, and fun
out of seeing our judgment vindicated, fun out of succeed-
ing.

What is success? How do we measure it? Well, our
measure of it is the extent to which our projects contribute
to the happiness and welfare of other people. That is more
important than money, although I am frank to admit that
we like to make a profit. Without it we couldn't keep going.

Maybe you think I am too optimistic in painting a bright picture of opportunities for success and happiness in the future. Well, I suppose I am an optimist and an idealist. But I also try to mix realism with my idealism. As I already have pointed out, I know the world is pretty chaotic and is headed toward a dark night instead of a pretty sunrise. But we can turn it around, and there is yet time to do it. We who are involved with the Here's Life Program of Campus Crusade are determined to help do it.

So I face the future with confidence. I believe that the United States is still the greatest country in the world and that under our free enterprise system there is no limit to where a person can go if he will seek God's will for his life and use his God-given talents to the fullest.

Well, I have given you my story as best I can. In closing, let me leave *you* with a challenge: Set goals for your life.

From the beginning, even before I knew the real value of it, goal-setting has been a way of life with me. Each day my goals are written down on a goal card, which I carry with me. Every goal is carefully thought out and prayed over.

As you write *your* goals, pray specifically that God will help you accomplish each goal you set for that day, week, month, or year. Then go to work to reach your goals, follow *your* burning desire for your life, and God will bless you richly.

Self-Help Guides
to Personal
Achievement

by W. Clement Stone

CHAPTER 5

1. Give your heart to God.
2. "Study to show thyself approved unto God, a workman that needeth not to be ashamed, rightly dividing the word of truth."— II Tim. 2:15
3. "Ask, and it shall be given you; seek, and ye shall find; knock, and it shall be opened unto you: For every one that asketh receiveth; and he that seeketh findeth; and to him that knocketh, it shall be opened."— Matt. 7:7–8
4. Grab opportunity when it comes.

CHAPTER 6

1. In adversity, keep praying to keep up hope.
2. See things through once you have started them.
3. Don't be a quitter.

CHAPTER 7

1. In advertising or writing, speak from your heart and from your own experience.
2. If you are unable to get a job, place a job-wanted ad in a leading newspaper.
3. Every adversity carries with it the seed of an equivalent or greater benefit.
4. Become an expert in your job.

CHAPTER 8

1. Keep dreaming and praying to achieve your goals.
2. With God's help, you cannot fail.
3. Use your goal as a self-help guide to achievement, as Wallace Johnson did with "A House a Day."
4. Share your good philosophy to improve the lives and habits of others.
5. To stay in business, be certain your sales prices develop profits.

CHAPTER 9

1. When in need, ask the Lord to guide you.
2. Loyalty is a virtue.
3. A secret for success is your home if God abides there.
4. When you have a goal, try to recognize that which will help you achieve it.

5. When you give your word, keep it.
6. Keep calm in an emergency.
7. When you go after something, don't come back until you get it.

CHAPTER 10

1. You don't always get what you expect unless you inspect.
2. "Ask, and it shall be given you; seek, and ye shall find; knock, and it shall be opened unto you."—Matt. 7:7
3. Take a personal interest in your employees, their families, and their problems.
4. Be a builder of men.
5. Like Wallace Johnson, turn lemons into lemonade.
6. Give prayers of thanks and prove your sincerity by sharing your blessings with the less fortunate.

CHAPTER 11

1. Develop a mastermind alliance with the experts you need.
2. In selling, turn a no into a yes with enthusiasm.
3. Have your money work for you daily.
4. If you are a person of proven character and meet your obligations, others will have faith in you.

CHAPTER 12

1. Before buying property for a business, remember that "location is all important."
2. Think big.
3. Recognize, relate, assimilate, and apply success principles.

CHAPTER 13

1. Work can be fun if you become an expert.
2. Plan your day and work your plan.
3. If you are a businessman, have an efficient secretary.
4. Use self-help motivational tapes to motivate you to high achievement.
5. Look for the message in a self-help book that is applicable to you.
6. Develop the proper attitude toward God, family, country, job, your fellowman—a positive, friendly, thankful attitude.

CHAPTER 14

1. In business, find a need and fill it.

2. Before engaging in any desirable activity, pray for guidance.

CHAPTER 15

1. The Golden Rule is to be lived, not just memorized.
2. Cultivate sincerity, honesty, friendliness, compassion, kindness, fairness, and humility.
3. Don't develop a credibility gap between you and others, be honest with everyone.
4. Good public relations are imperative for continuous success.
5. Remember, every human being has feelings, emotions, and problems. Be sensitive to the potential reactions of others by watching what you say and how you say it.

CHAPTER 16

1. "And we know that all things work together for good to them that love God, to them who are the called according to his purpose."— Rom. 8:28
2. Remember, God is always a good God. Continue to have faith.
3. "Our happiness has never been dependent on money. Happiness comes from within, from the right attitude toward God and toward one another, from work that you enjoy doing, from having worthwhile goals and striving toward them, from helping people and good causes all along the way."
4. Thank God for giving you the wisdom to make a livelihood, but pray earnestly for the wisdom to use your money properly.
5. Honest work and thrift are not below the dignity of any man.

CHAPTER 17

1. Habits and ambitions formed as children may become a way of life.
2. If it is necessary to disagree, do so in a manner that is not disagreeable.
3. There is no substitute for hard work. The American dream is not dead as long as we are willing to work. Freedom to work is second only to religious freedom.

CHAPTER 18

1. Once the government takes over anything, it's hard to get the government to turn loose.
2. With a positive mental attitude and the help of God, difficulties can be turned into advantages.

CHAPTER 19

1. When you go into partnership, be certain of the honesty and integrity as well as the ability of the person you select.
2. Wallace Johnson accepted the challenge of Here's Life for the purpose of making this world a better world for this and for future generations. What are you doing to make your world a better world? You can become involved in Here's Life or in other opportunities in line with your philosophy.
3. Engage in soul-searching, in praying, and in thinking time.
4. What the mind of man can conceive and believe, the mind of man can achieve with the help of God.

CHAPTER 20

1. The greatest threat to our democracy and to our way of life is that of having wrong attitudes toward God, country, flag, families, jobs, people who don't agree with us, morality, honesty, and persons of other religious faiths or ethnic groups.
2. In your thinking time, don't overlook your shortcomings, try to correct them.
3. The essence of perfection is never reached, but one becomes more perfect by trying.

CHAPTER 21

1. Grow old along with me! The best is yet to be."—Robert Browning
2. "Jesus said, . . . all things are possible to him that believeth." —Mark 9:23
3. They are rich who have love for God, for their children, for their fellowmen, and who are persons of industry, honesty, integrity, and general good character.
4. If you are married, be as kind and thoughtful to your spouse as . you were in the early days of your marriage.
5. Opportunities today are unlimited for those who recognize, understand, and apply the self-help guides contained in this book.
6. Wallace Johnson communicated with his Senior Silent Partner frequently every day. You can, too.